Commish & the Cardinals

The most memorable games, as covered by
Hall of Famer Rick Hummel of the St. Louis Post-Dispatch

Editor
Mike Smith

Art direction / design
Wade Wilson

Photo editor
Larry Coyne

Writer
Rick Hummel

Contributing writer
Bernie Miklasz

Assistant Photo Editor
Hillary Levin

Contributing copy editor
Curtis Peck

Sales and marketing
Gail LaFata

Special thanks to Doug Weaver of Kansas City Star Books, and to the St. Louis Cardinals

Softcover
ISBN978-0-9661397-9-2

Printed by Walsworth Publishing Co., Marceline, Mo.

To order additional copies, call **1-800-329-0224**
Order online at **www.post-dispatchstore.com**

CONTENTS

4 • There's Only One Commish

12 • The Games

To commemorate his 30 seasons as a baseball writer for the Post-Dispatch, here are 30 of the most memorable Cardinals games and events covered by Rick Hummel. Each account includes Hummel's original story from the Post-Dispatch, plus "Commish's Moment," his reminiscence about the event.

214 • The Extras

Excerpts of Hummel stories from an additional 10 memorable games.

224 • Credits

ABOUT THE COMMISH

Hummel in 1978

A native of Quincy, Ill., and a University of Missouri graduate, Rick Hummel began working for the Post-Dispatch in 1971 after a three-year stint in the Army. He covered everything from high school football to Spirits of St. Louis pro basketball to the boxing Spinks brothers, until he became the Cardinals beat writer in 1978. Hummel has been the baseball columnist for the Post-Dispatch since 2002. Along the way, he picked up the nickname by which he is known throughout baseball: Commish.

Hummel covered the Cardinals' 1982 and 2006 World Series championship teams, and has chronicled three National League MVPs, eight managers and five NL pennant winners. His writing career has bridged Bob Gibson to Chris Carpenter, Lou Brock to Albert Pujols and Red Schoendienst to Tony La Russa, and has taken him to 27 All-Star Games and 29 World Series.

In December 2006, Hummel won the J.G. Taylor Spink Award "for meritorious contributions to baseball writing" and with it, induction into the writers' wing of the National Baseball Hall of Fame. On July 29, 2007, Commish will become the third Post-Dispatch writer to enter the Hall of Fame, joining former sports editors Bob Broeg and J. Roy Stockton.

The "Commish," Rick Hummel, goes over notes and reviews his scorebook before covering a game at Busch Stadium in 2005.

THERE'S ONLY ONE COMMISH

BY BERNIE MIKLASZ • POST-DISPATCH SPORTS COLUMNIST

ONE NIGHT IN MILWAUKEE, baseball writer Tom Haudricourt, who covers the Brewers for the Journal Sentinel, entered the County Stadium press box, spotted an old friend and hollered, "Hey, Commish!"

Bud Selig turned around. Which is natural, because Selig is the commissioner of baseball, he lives in Milwaukee, and he has known Haudricourt for 25 years.

Except that Haudricourt wasn't talking to Selig.

Instead, he pointed to Post-Dispatch baseball writer Rick Hummel, who was seated near Selig.

Sorry, Bud.

In any baseball press box in North America, there is only one Commish, and it is Hummel. In the land of the laptops, Hummel rules as perhaps the most respected baseball writer of his generation.

About that nickname: It stems from Hummel's remarkable grasp of ordinances. A long time ago, members of the Post-Dispatch sports department formed a tabletop, dice-and-charts-based football league, and only Hummel could decipher the rules of the hopelessly complex game. So he was appointed league commissioner. And his term was extended many times over, as Hummel organized bowling and softball teams at the newspaper.

Hummel also became something of a parliamentarian when sportswriters and broadcasters and assorted friends set up the usual office pools for big sporting events.

Through the years, though, Hummel's nickname evolved into a different meaning. It came to represent his status in the baseball writing profession, and the vast admiration he engenders from his colleagues. I don't believe there's ever been a baseball writer more beloved by his peers than

Rick Hummel. I could be wrong, but as Tony La Russa would say, at the very least Hummel is tied for first.

Traveling with Hummel, I've watched a familiar scene played out many times. He'd enter the stadiums in New York or Los Angeles and all the places in between, and the ballwriters would light up in his presence. Grizzled, cynical, weary baseball scribes stopped what they were doing to walk over and greet Hummel. He's such a friendly, warm person, devoid of agendas or motives or ego. And Hummel's cordial personality lifted the mood in any press box. Understand that baseball writers are generally grumpy people who trudge through a long season short on sleep, deep in lousy press-box food, and slammed tight against crazy deadlines. But Hummel usually makes them smile. When Montreal had a baseball team, Hummel's arrival at Olympic Stadium was that of a visiting dignitary from a foreign land; they all but rolled out a red carpet.

Hummel was treated like a Hall of Fame baseball writer years before it became official. Our Commish is the latest recipient of the J.G. Taylor Spink Award for contributions to baseball writing. The honor was inevitable, because Hummel carried on the Post-Dispatch's impressive history of distinctive baseball writing. And he follows J. Roy Stockton and Bob Broeg into Cooperstown. The tradition continues, and Hummel is the rightful heir to the Stockton-Broeg legacy. Especially Broeg, who hired Hummel, and cherished him. We only wish the late BB could be on that stage when Hummel joins him in Cooperstown.

A great baseball town isn't a great baseball town without great baseball writers. I believe Hummel is one of the reasons why St. Louis is such an intelligent haven for baseball knowledge and discussion. More than anything, fans here know the game because it runs deep in the collective mind-set. It really is a way of life, a connection that binds the generations. A youngster growing up as a Cardinal fan has had plenty of baseball teachers along the way, whether it be a parent, a grandparent, siblings, cousins, neighbors, etc. And for more than a quarter-century, Hummel has played a role in enhancing the baseball IQ with his highly detailed, touch-all-bases game stories. If you want the game deftly analyzed without an ego attack of flowery, excessive writing, Hummel is your guy.

And he has a way of calmly looking at things in a way that lowers the temperature, and reduces the bluster. I can't tell you how many times I've bellowed in the press box about some manager's apparent bonehead move, only to have Hummel thoughtfully point out the reason why the move made sense. Hummel, who quietly watches games, doesn't miss a thing. He can identify the nuances and subtleties that elude otherwise intelligent writers,

A pair of commissioners, Hummel and Bud Selig, exchange pleasantries at the 2007 Baseball Writers Dinner in St. Louis.

and fans. I learned something every day sitting next to this man.

And the readers learned by scanning the copy under Hummel's trusted byline. If a reader wanted to know why Whitey Herzog pulled a pitcher, or why an umpire seemingly missed a call, or why La Russa allowed his starting pitcher to hit in the eighth inning – don't worry. Hummel had the explanation in the next edition of the Post-Dispatch. Commish gets the best answers because the people in the game view him as a man who knows baseball, and they often respond as if talking to a peer.

Herzog offered the best testimonial: He's dealt with hundreds of writers through the years, but of all the scribes, Herzog said Hummel asked the most intelligent questions, and had the sharpest eye for detail. Hummel, like his late mentor, Mr. Broeg, also has a baseball encyclopedia stored in his brain. Hummel's instant recall of game situations from some contest played years ago is simply astounding. I can't even remember what happened in the third inning of the game I'm watching today, and Commish can tell you about the third inning of a game played in 1987.

Most of this is Hummel, but at least some of it was handed down. Hummel's sense of baseball history, and Cardinals history, was enriched by Broeg, the classic storyteller. From the underrated Neal Russo, who manned the Cardinals beat before Hummel, Rick learned the importance of building relationships in the clubhouse, and the best way of dealing with players and managers and adjusting to their moods. Hummel moves easily in a clubhouse. Players, managers and coaches appreciate him for his polite, professional and persistent line of interrogation. He is not one to waste their time.

The writer-player working dynamic has deteriorated through the years, in part because few writers possess Hummel's gentlemanly instincts. In all of his seasons covering ball, Hummel has had only three unpleasant conflicts. Pitcher John Denny for some reason berated Hummel because of a photo caption that Hummel had nothing to do with. Catcher Steve Swisher noisily protested Hummel's "D" grade on a season-ending report card, only to have Hummel coolly point to Swisher's .173 batting average. And a hot-headed umpire once accused Hummel of using an off-the-record quote – a preposterous accusation, considering Rick's high standard of integrity. Sure enough, the umpire recanted and apologized a few days later.

Hummel also got along famously with so-called grumpy players, such as "Silent" George Hendrick, Jack Clark, Mark McGwire, Garry Templeton, Vince Coleman. Ozzie Smith could be crabby with Hummel, but they always made peace. Bob Gibson always returns Hummel's calls. The best example was Joaquin Andujar, who mostly refused to speak to reporters, except for his profanity-laced command to stay away. Andujar generally despised baseball writers, but liked Hummel and treated him with courtesy.

Why do the players and the managers like Hummel? It isn't because he's soft. It isn't because he covered up bad news. But he doesn't have a bombastic, attention-seeking style of writing. Don't confuse that with passivity. Players have viewed Hummel as a responsible and fair writer who wouldn't burn them in an effort to generate noisy, self-promoting headlines. Hummel doesn't shoot for controversy in his stories. He just writes what he sees, writes what he knows, and talks to people to fill in the blanks in his stories. And then he crafts a complete account. He's accurate in his use of quotes. This understated style benefits the readers, because Hummel has uninterrupted access to the athletes, who tell him things that they won't tell other media people.

Another thing that makes Hummel special is his longevity, his willingness to devote his adult life to the demands of covering the game that he loves. I don't expect nonwriters to understand this, but the daily baseball beat is a demanding and consuming challenge. Those who choose this

▲ Hummel does the honors in changing the countdown board as Busch Stadium's final days are marked. A different celebrity connected with a particular number tears off the appropriate number at each game in 2005. Hummel began covering the Cardinals full time in 1978.

career path are required to make a personal sacrifice, at least if they plan on doing their jobs well. The hours are brutal, the days off rare, and the travel relentless. And even when a writer like Hummel is "home" he's not really there much, because his schedule doesn't mesh with family and other loved ones.

The baseball life can be fun, and a real adventure. Hummel collected friends in every NL city, and my favorite was Phil the Thrill, the Commish's personal taxi driver in Cincinnati. But the road life is also a wearing and damaging experience. That's why, when young writers take on a baseball beat today, they usually make a deal with an editor, and cap their length of service, agreeing to the assignment for two or three years. Understand that Hummel covered the Cardinals virtually every day for 24 seasons, and had a major share of the beat for six other seasons. That's an incredible number of miles, hotel rooms and days away from home.

And while no longer grinding away on the road, Hummel still spends more than 100 days a year in baseball stadiums. Among the writers, he's usually among the first to arrive, and among the last to leave. I can't imagine his word count over the years — we have to be talking hundreds of thousands of words, or into the millions. Cardinals fans were fortunate to hear the words of Jack Buck on the radio, and then wake up and read Hummel's words in print.

Rick, in some ways, is a survivor. There is a personal price to pay for all of these endless road trips, a price to pay for being the eternal boy of baseball's summer. Rick would be the first to volunteer that the baseball life disrupted his home life in a way that couldn't be repaired by a couple of months off during the winter. He'd be the first to tell you that the good times on the road can easily lead to some corrosive habits.

Commish led so many expeditions to the writers' hangout, the Missouri Bar & Grille, that he quips he might have to wear one of the saloon's hats into Cooperstown, in the same way that a player chooses a hat of a team to be depicted on his official Cooperstown plaque. But here's the serious follow-up to that joke: Hummel had the strength of character to change his lifestyle, and he hasn't sipped anything stronger than club soda for many years. And of the many things colleagues and friends love about Rick, we are probably most proud of the way he took control of his life. It had to be extremely difficult, but he did it, and we respect him more than ever for it.

Hummel also has an old-school charm that's irresistible. He has an 80-degree rule for his ballpark dress code. If the temperature at game time is below 80 degrees, he wears a tie. If it's 80 or higher, the tie comes off. Baseball writers tend to be a little on the eccentric side. Russo was a highly educated and brilliant man, who could do crossword puzzles in Latin. But he also hauled around a bag of trinkets, gizmos and snacks that he'd sell to co-workers, calling his side business "NR Products." Once, at a charity softball game featuring Cardinals players, Russo sat near the dugout and inexplicably began to set off fireworks, cherry bombs and other explosives that he pulled from his "NR Products" bag. Cardinals pitcher Bob Forsch turned to Hummel and said, "That's you 25 years from now."

Until recently, Hummel has engaged in open warfare with modern technology. For years he lugged a cumbersome, heavy, and unsightly computerized contraption around the nation, banging out stories on the thing long after other writers switched to lighter and more efficient laptops. Hummel's dinosaur machine kept crashing, and with the help of the newspaper's technical-support staff, which went to a computer graveyard for used parts, he'd stubbornly find a way to revive the dead machine. It finally perished, could not be saved, and Hummel had to convert to the modern world. It wasn't easy at first. When pressed with a technological difficulty, Hummel's response is to start slapping the computer and berating it. It's the only time I ever see this cheerful man in a foul mood. And when Hummel spars three rounds with a laptop, other Post-Dispatch writers chuckle but cover our faces, because we don't want him to get mad at us.

For years, Hummel drove an Oscar Madison tribute car — a remarkable clunker loaded down with media guides, press releases, ancient newspapers, and quite possibly the Dead Sea Scrolls. To make matters worse, the passenger-side door wouldn't open from the outside. And the back seat was filled with Hummel's traveling library. So if you needed a ride, you had to crawl in from the driver's side, or enter the vehicle from a back door and somehow scale the mountain of newspapers to climb into the front seat. I wonder if anyone ever checked for Jimmy Hoffa back there?

Hummel drives a nice car now. And lo and behold, he's even doing audio reports for the Post-Dispatch website, STLtoday.com. He's become friendly with new media, a thoroughly modern man. He even enjoys looking up things on the Internet now. This is simply incomprehensible, like Musial batting righthanded.

The Commish has come a long way from his high school days in Quincy, Ill. This career started when he informed his driver's education teacher, Melvin Tappe, of his desire to become a sports broadcaster. Tappe discouraged the notion, suggesting that most broadcasting jobs would go to former athletes. Tappe suggested sportswriting instead. Hummel took the advice. He didn't know how to type, so he'd write out his early stories, longhand, and his mom would type them up for the school paper. The next semester, Hummel took a typing class, and was on his way to Cooperstown. I just wish the other writers could carry him in. Because he's been carrying us, and our newspaper, for more than a quarter century.

In January, when Hummel and other Hall of Famers and award winners were honored at a black-tie affair in the grand ballroom of a classy hotel, a group of prominent Cardinals bought a page in the dinner program.

"Congratulations Rick," the salute stated. "Welcome to the shrine. Stop in when you're in town. We're just down the hall."

It was signed by Cardinal Hall of Famers Lou Brock, Bob Gibson, Stan Musial, Bruce Sutter, Ozzie Smith and Red Schoendienst.

This swing gives Lou Brock his 3,000th hit, a single. It comes off Cubs righthander Dennis Lamp in a game at Busch Stadium.

AUG. 13 1979 — BROCK'S 3,000TH HIT

LOU BROCK SAID THAT IT HAD TURNED OUT just about the way he had fantasized it, this 3,000th hit. "I pictured in my mind a hit up the middle," he said. "But I didn't know Dennis Lamp was going to get in the way of it."

At 8:50 p.m. as a Busch Stadium crowd of 46,161 erupted in a fourth-

inning frenzy, Brock, in his second at-bat, lashed his second hit of the game. It was a single off the hand of Lamp, the Chicago Cubs' pitcher. Third baseman Steve Ontiveros clutched the ball but had no play as Brock skittered across first base and into the record books. The Cardinals left fielder became only the 14th player to reach the 3,000-hit milestone.

There ensued an immediate ceremony at which Cardinals president August A. Busch Jr. and Stan Musial, the only other Cardinal with 3,000 hits, spoke briefly. Musial presented Brock the ball in play on his 3,000th hit 21 years ago, and then Brock talked.

"You fans here deserved to see the 3,000th hit," Brock said. "Stan came extremely close but didn't quite make it (Musial had his 3,000th hit in Chicago). Mr. Busch said, 'You're going to do it here.' I said, 'I am?' "

Brock did, putting the finishing touches on what he called "orchestrating my own exodus."

"I've always wanted to leave baseball in a blaze of glory," Brock said. "I've always wanted to orchestrate my own exodus and I'm doing a pretty good job of it."

If that sounds immodest, consider that Brock's pride had suffered severe contusions during the 1978 season, when he hit a dismal .221. At that point, there were serious doubts raised as to whether he could amass the 100 hits necessary to reach 3,000. Was he washed up?

"You guys (the media) said that, I didn't," Brock said. "One-hundred hits is not an awful lot of hits to get, provided you get a chance to play."

Brock noted that the Cardinals organization "had looked for a replacement for me for the last two years and the third year it turned out to be me."

But he said the 3,000 plateau "had not been an obsession. The most important thing was to crown my career with a fine performance," Brock said. "Three-thousand hits was a star in that crown."

It was with some irony that Brock achieved the milestone. The Cubs were the ones who signed Brock in 1961 but traded him in 1964. Brock's first homer had come off the Cardinals in 1962. His 3,000th hit had come off the hand that first fed him.

However, Brock said, "It didn't matter to me whether I got it against somebody from the moon or Mars or some other ballclub. (The Cubs) just happened to be in town."

The main impetus for the historic hit probably was provided by Lamp, who zipped a one-ball, two-strike fastball under Brock's chin.

"Once a ball gets under my chin, that makes me nervous," said Brock. "It was a close call." But once Lamp got Brock's attention, Brock

Teammates congratulate the future Hall of Famer on his hitting feat.

got Lamp's. On the next pitch, Brock literally knocked the Cubs righthander from the mound with his line drive. Lamp suffered bruises on three fingers on his pitching hand.

Putting things in some perspective, Brock, after being taken out of the game in the fifth inning, walked to the room where Lamp was undergoing X-rays to check the extent of the injury.

There had been an air of almost astonishing casualness before the game. Brock arrived leisurely about 5:30, two hours before the game, and responded before anyone had asked him, "No, I'm not nervous."

But the barbs from teammates came anyway. "What have you got to be nervous about?" challenged Garry Templeton. "You've got nothing to be nervous about." The two then shadow-boxed briefly and Brock went about the business of "getting my wheels" pumped up by trainer Gene Gieselmann.

Ken Reitz brought up a bet he had made with Brock in spring training. A steak dinner rode on whether Reitz got to 1,000 hits before Brock got to 3,000. Reitz needed only one hit, which he got in the ninth inning, but that was much too late. He will be buying Brock dinner when the team gets to San Francisco.

Bob Forsch offered, "What if they fill this place up and then they announce that Lou isn't going to play tonight, that he might play tomorrow?"

Brock calmly spoke of plans to donate $1 for every hit to an organization to be announced later, and then began rolling tape around a bat. He rolled five pieces, an inch or so apart, around the bat and said that pitcher Silvio Martinez, of all people, had given him the idea.

"I went into spring training with no margin for error," said Brock. "I didn't want my hands to slip on the bat." With the tape, Brock assured himself that his hands wouldn't slip. The only problem, he said, was that somebody kept taking his bats. He had to use somebody else's.

There followed a foray into the equipment room where Brock saw no bats marked "No. 20" in the rack. But a batboy said, "Oh, your bats are locked up over here." Sure enough, Brock, to his surprise, found a dozen or so bats and he extracted four.

But, as fate would have it, Brock said afterward he had no idea what bat he used to reach 3,000. It may not even have been his own.

It didn't really matter. Wife Virgie was there and so were children Wanda, Louis Jr., little Emory and littler Daniel Christopher (11 days old). Those who weren't asleep beamed as a perspiring Brock faced a phalanx of newsmen.

Brock said that Al Kaline, the former Detroit Tigers star who sent one of the congratulatory telegrams, was the first to instill in his mind the prospect of getting 3,000 hits. "He said, 'You've got a chance . . .' But he said it wasn't going to be easy," related Brock.

In the spring of 1973, Brock, who had 2,001 hits at that point, told Post-Dispatch Sports Editor Bob Broeg that the prospect was "remote."

But, Brock said, ultimately 3,000 came within range. I woke up one morning and I was only 300 hits away from it."

It wasn't quite that simple, though, as he then readily pointed out. "Unfortunately, 1977 and 1978 were not part of the plan," he said.

That's when the whispers of Brock being washed up started. Now those whispers have been washed away.

After hitting .304 and getting his 3,000th hit in 1979,
Brock decides to call it a career.

COMMISH'S MOMENT

BROCK'S 3,000TH HIT was one of the highlights of a career that some had presumed to be over the season before. Yanked in and out of the lineup by manager Vern Rapp, Brock batted .221 in 1978. So I had written a piece myself, suggesting that Brock could be nearing the end of the line.

Approachable by almost anybody else but upset by the tack I had taken, Brock decided he wouldn't be talking to me the rest of the season.

Imagine how I felt, in my first full season on the beat, having alienated one of the most popular Cardinals of all time. But we worked it out the following spring in Florida.

AUG. 26 1981 | TEMPLETON'S MELTDOWN

WHEN THE CARDINALS' CHARTERED FLIGHT from St. Louis landed in San Diego late Wednesday night, there seemed to be an overriding consensus that no one much cared if Garry Templeton, their tempestuous and suspended shortstop, came back or not.

"I've bent over backward and I've been in his corner a long time," said one player. "But this is incredibly ridiculous. What he did was embarrassing to me and the fans."

Templeton was ejected amid a stream of obscene actions in Wednesday afternoon's game in St. Louis.

The "Ladies Day" crowd at Busch Stadium booed Templeton in the first inning of a game with the San Francisco Giants when he failed to run toward first base on a dropped third strike. Templeton responded with a raised finger.

The fans continued to boo him as he ran off the field after the second inning, and some fans reportedly were making obscene gestures toward Templeton. Jeers and boos rained down on Templeton as he was ejected from the game, and he responded with another series of obscene gestures.

To a man, the players applauded Manager Whitey Herzog's action of grabbing Templeton by the shirt as if he were a bad-apple schoolboy and dragging him off the field and into the dugout. Any fine and subsequent suspension won't be as significant as Herzog's initial reaction was.

"I could have kissed Whitey for that. He couldn't have done it better," said one player.

Herzog said he was a bit embarrassed by what happened. "I'm not proud of what I did, but I had to do it," he said. "I just don't understand the boy. He's trying to disrupt the whole ballclub."

Most players interviewed did not want to be quoted by name, but most seemed quite satisfied that backup shortstop Mike Ramsey would be a

◄ Shortstop Garry Templeton makes one of a series of obscene gestures to a Ladies Day crowd during a game with the San Francisco Giants at Busch Stadium.

more than adequate replacement.

"We can win with Ramsey," said catcher Gene Tenace. "At least you'll know he'll give you 100 percent. With Templeton, you never knew. You never knew if he'd even talk to you or not."

Ramsey understandably was reluctant to comment on what could be his good fortune.

"I want to play, but this is an unfortunate situation," Ramsey said. "I would like to get into his head and find out what he's thinking."

Many players said they had gone about as far as they could with Templeton's emotional cycle.

"He's an idiot," said one, flatly.

"He's goofy, he's crazy," said another.

"If he comes back," said another player, "I don't know what's going to happen in the clubhouse. He's done something you just don't do.

"I don't know if he'll come back. I hope he doesn't."

Templeton did not accompany the team on Wednesday night's flight.

Tenace said, "I don't think he'll have the guts to come back." It was a sentiment several other Cardinals offered.

"He's played his last game here," said one player. "He's dug his grave."

Somehow, Herzog said wanly, he didn't expect that it would be long before he heard from Templeton. "He's losing $4,200 a day," Herzog said.

"I feel sorry for the kid," said Herzog. "I think he needs some help."

Manager Whitey Herzog pulls Templeton into the dugout after an obscene gesture leads to the player's ejection from the game by umpire Bruce Froemming.

COMMISH'S MOMENT

TEMPLETON HAD JUST COME BACK INTO THE LINEUP the night before after being out with a leg injury. After he had gone one for five, manager Whitey Herzog told him to be careful when he was running the bases the next afternoon. But not that careful.

When Templeton struck out in the first inning, he apparently was unaware that the ball had eluded the catcher and had headed to the backstop. Templeton belatedly began a jog to first and was thrown out.

On a hot day, the fans were none too pleased, and some near the field began throwing ice at him besides booing him. Templeton complained to home-plate Bruce Froemming on a couple of occasions and, finally, after Templeton grabbed his crotch in response to the fans, Froemming had seen enough and ejected him.

So, too, had Herzog, who pulled Templeton down the dugout steps.

AUG. 22 1982 BRUMMER'S MAD DASH

MORE THAN AN HOUR AFTER THE FACT, Keith Hernandez sat in a glazed state of wonderment. "I thought I had seen it all," he said. "I have not seen it all.

"I'll probably never see that again in my career. Stealing home plate with two strikes and two outs . . . I'll never see that again."

Hernandez was as overcome as everyone else in Busch Stadium — and that covers 46,827 paying spectators, both managers, the third-base coach and all the other players on both teams — when Glenn Brummer stole home with two outs and two strikes on David Green, giving the Cardinals a 5-4 victory in 12 innings over the San Francisco Giants.

Glenn Brummer is a catcher for the Cardinals, about once a month anyway. Before getting a single to lead off the 12th, he had not had a hit since July 16 and only one since June 19. He plays normally only when Manager Whitey Herzog is about to run out of players, as he did Sunday, when Dane Iorg became a father for the fifth time and spent the day at the hospital.

"I never would have thought that I'd steal home in my career," said Brummer. "It's like a dream come true that a catcher would try to steal home for the St. Louis Cardinals or anybody else to win a ballgame."

Herzog sanctions such a play — "we tell them that if they think they can can make it, to go ahead" — but trying to steal home with two outs and a 1-2 count violates most, if not all, unwritten rules of baseball.

"A hitter has got to protect the strike zone. You've got to give your hitter a chance to swing the bat with two strikes," said Tom Herr, who has stolen home twice himself.

"It was just one of those plays. It was an unexpected thing and an unexpected guy to do it."

Given Herzog's bold use of suicide squeezes, one would have thought he had choreographed this mad dash, also. But the manager said, "Nobody

Second baseman Tom Herr catches Glenn Brummer, who is jumping for joy after his game-winning steal of home in the 12th inning against the San Francisco Giants.

knew he was coming. I didn't, either."

Not unexpectedly, the Giants offered a wild argument at game's end. Their main point was that the pitch to Green might well have been strike three, in which case it wouldn't have mattered if Brummer had scored. "If it's strike three, it's no run," said home plate umpire Dave Pallone.

But Pallone, who, according to a television replay, stepped to the left of the plate to make his decision, said he called the pitch from lefthander Gary Lavelle a ball and that catcher Milt May hadn't disputed that issue.

"May asked me if the guy had gotten under the tag," Pallone said. The rest of the Giants, led by Manager Frank Robinson and pitching coach Don McMahon "were arguing that I hadn't called the pitch. I called it a ball," Pallone reaffirmed.

"(Expletive)," said Robinson.

"He hasn't called anything," Robinson said. "He wasn't even behind the plate when the ball got to the plate. He didn't call a ball. He didn't call anything. He's a liar."

Hernandez said he could understand an umpire's confusion on the play. "He had a vapor lock," Hernandez said. "He was just as surprised as anybody in the ballpark."

Let us take you now to that twilight ride of Glenn Brummer. There was no "one if by land, two if by sea." There were no signs at all.

"I was thinking about it all the time but I didn't want to tip it off," said Brummer. "I took my normal lead on three of the pitches. On the second and third pitch, I noticed there was a lot of high leg kick in his stretch. If he has a high leg kick, he's taking some time to get rid of the ball. I got to a certain point where I knew they were not going to pick me off. I think I was 30 feet off. I just kept edging, edging. Slowly, slowly. When he stretched, I just went."

Green alertly picked up Brummer just in time. "He was so close. I had to get out of the way. He almost broke my ankle."

Brummer shows off the home plate he received as a memento of his memorable theft. The drawing is by Amadee, a Post-Dispatch artist, and the signatures are those of Cardinals players and others in the Cardinals organization.

COMMISH'S MOMENT

IT WAS A HOT, SULTRY SUNDAY AFTERNOON at Busch Stadium and Brummer, nicknamed "Tractorhead" by his teammates, decided to take matters into his own hands when he found himself at third base with the bases loaded and two out in the 12th.

Early in the count to David Green, Brummer told veteran third-base coach Chuck Hiller he thought he could steal home on high-kicking Gary Lavelle. Hiller talked Brummer out of it — until with two strikes on Green, Brummer took off. Hiller was as flabbergasted as any of the 46,000 in the ballpark. "With two strikes?" Hiller said later. "I've never seen that done before."

Flushed with the success of his game-winning theft, Brummer tried to steal twice more during the season before manager Whitey Herzog took his green light away.

SEPT. 14 1982 | SUTTER-SCHMIDT SHOWDOWN

PHILADELPHIA

JOHN STUPER HAD DONE MORE THAN HIS SHARE to create the ultimate matchup. The Cardinals' rookie had pitched 7 1/3 scoreless innings, permitting just four hits. It was time, with a 2-0 Cardinals lead, to yield to Bruce Sutter.

There were runners at first and second with one out when Philadelphia's Gary Matthews hit a ball between shortstop and third that Cardinals third baseman Ken Oberkfell gloved with a diving stop. But, after hesitating when he looked to second, Obie's throw to first was too late to get Matthews. Bases loaded and as Mike Shannon would say, "Ol' Abner's done it again."

The Phillies' Mike Schmidt was at the plate.

More than 32,000 fans in Veterans Stadium, lulled to sleep by the mastery of Stuper and the Phillies' Mike Krukow, had awakened with a din. Stuper, a rookie experiencing his first real pennant race, was as enthralled as the rest. "That confrontation between Sutter and Schmidt . . . that is what baseball is all about," he said. And he was right. The Cardinals' 2-0 victory was extraordinary.

Said Sutter of the mighty Schmidt: "I honestly feel he's the best hitter in the league. The last two years, it seems to me he's hit a lot of home runs when they needed them."

Indeed, but Sutter's split-fingered fastball was at its explosive, dive-bombing best as he got two quick strikes on Schmidt. Then, after Schmidt had worked the count to 2-2, Sutter got Schmidt to tap to the mound, where the Cardinals pitcher started a home-to-first double play that preserved the lead.

 Relief ace Bruce Sutter provides a number of exciting moments for Cardinals fans during the 1982 pennant race, but few more memorable than the game in which he induces Phillies slugger Mike Schmidt to hit into an inning-ending, bases-loaded double play.

Afterward, emerging in a cloud of talcum powder after showering, Schmidt addressed the significance of the duel.

"He's at his best when the hitter has a lot of pressure on him," said Schmidt of Sutter. "The first couple of swings, I jumped at it too much. Then, a tap back to the mound. I'd have been better off striking out. I've hit into a pitcher-to- home-to-first double play maybe once in 10 years. I've had a pretty good average against him (this season, two doubles in two at-bats) but it didn't mean diddly-squat tonight.

"But it was fun . . . facing the best relief pitcher in the league with the ball-game on the line. He won our little battle tonight. I hope it happens tomorrow (Schmidt chuckled) with an eight-run lead. It was one heckuva at-bat. I'll probably have some trouble getting to sleep tonight thinking about it."

When the Phillies went to the field in the ninth inning, it was obvious Schmidt, who almost always emits an aura of cool, was thinking about the at-bat. He placed his cap sideways on his head, much like baseball clown Max Patkin. He angrily flashed his hand through the dirt at third base and indiscriminately fired pebbles.

When the Cardinals' Mike Ramsey hit a liner to his right in the ninth, Schmidt casually backhanded it, a play that only he might have made, and he didn't even have his heart in it.

There are 19 games more for the Cardinals this season and 18 for the Phillies but there will be few that are more dramatic than this one.

"I just sit there and watch it," said Cardinals Manager Whitey Herzog. "I just about puke a lot of times. But what are you going to do? You've just got to hope."

Catcher Darrell Porter, who had provided the two runs with a fourth-inning homer, said Sutter's magic pitch was the best he had seen in awhile. Sutter concurred. "The way they were swinging and the way they were reacting, it must have been breaking pretty big," Sutter said.

"But when I'm throwing the ball well, I don't see the ball break. My head is bouncing. When I see my ball break, when I see it roll, then I'm in trouble."

COMMISH'S MOMENT

SUTTER'S CRITICAL DOUBLE PLAY on Schmidt was pennant-race baseball at its best. The showdown came a night after the Phillies had gone ahead by half a game over the Cardinals in the National League East when former Cardinal Steve Carlton struck out 12 and hit a homer to beat Bob Forsch 2-0.

After Sutter preserved John Stuper's lead to win 2-0 and put the Cardinals back up by one-half game, they clobbered another ex-Cardinal, John Denny, 8-0 in the series finale. Then it was on to New York, where they stretched out their division lead by winning five games in three days against the hapless Mets.

All in all, an interesting three days in Philadelphia. The sideshows included an early-morning fire that routed the sleeping Cardinals from their hotel; fans pelting outfielder Lonnie Smith with a rum bottle, a beer can and coins after some horse-play with the Phillie Phanatic; and Denny issuing an oral position paper on why he doesn't talk to reporters.

OCT. 20 1982 — CELEBRATION! CARDS WIN SERIES

THE LAST TIME THE CARDINALS WON THE WORLD CHAMPIONSHIP of baseball, Lyndon B. Johnson was president, the split-fingered fastball hadn't been invented and most baseball teams still played on God's green earth instead of that artificial stuff. The year was 1967, and some of the heroes were Bob Gibson, Lou Brock, Tim McCarver, Orlando Cepeda and Mike Shannon.

At 10:17 p.m. on Oct. 20, 1982, Joaquin Andujar, Bruce Sutter, Keith Hernandez, Darrell Porter, Tom Herr, a couple of guys named Smith and a varied cast of achievers, overachievers and good company men assumed their own spots in Cardinals World Series lore.

It was then that Sutter, the art's leading practitioner of split-fingered pitching, blew a non-split-fingered fastball past the swing of a startled Gorman Thomas and the Cardinals closed out a 6-3 victory over the Milwaukee Brewers in the seventh game of the 1982 World Series.

The Cardinals had trailed the Brewers, three games to two, when they returned to Busch Stadium after having lost two of three games in Wisconsin last weekend. But the Redbirds pounded out 27 hits here the last two nights, including 15 in Game Seven when they overcame a 3-1 Milwaukee lead with a three-run rally in the sixth inning.

Only three of their number — Gene Tenace, George Hendrick and Lonnie Smith — ever had experienced the euphoria of the moment. As champagne was sprayed and the sponsor's product was consumed in large quantities, most of the Cardinals said they wouldn't really know the true essence until several days later, but they knew the feeling was a powerful one.

"The only thing that would compare to it," said Herr, "was being in the delivery room the day that our son, Aaron, was born. That was an awesome feeling."

Catcher Darrell Porter, named the series' Most Valuable Player, said the

Bruce Sutter celebrates after striking out Brewers slugger Gorman Thomas to end Game 7 and give the Cards the World Series championship.

thrill of this victory ranked somewhere behind sobriety, God, his marriage and the birth of his daughter, but "it was flat-out fun."

The city was plunged into a nightlong celebration that was to continue the next day with a downtown parade. The Cardinals have won nine world championships, but 15 years had been a long time to wait.

For Gussie Busch, the Cardinals owner, it indeed was the "one more championship for the great fans of St. Louis" that he had hoped for. "I've never been happier in my whole life," said Busch in a madhouse locker room. "I was sure this team could win it, and it didn't let me down."

It was the first world championship for his manager, Whitey Herzog, who had three division winners as manager of the Kansas City Royals. "I feel about as good as you can feel," said Herzog. "I'm happy for Mr. Busch, the greatest man in the world."

It didn't come easily.

Former Cardinal Pete Vuckovich, having stranded nine runners through the first five innings, nursed a 3-1 Milwaukee lead into the bottom of the sixth inning. With one out, Ozzie Smith stroked a single to left and Lonnie Smith doubled down the third-base line, past a diving Paul Molitor.

Milwaukee Manager Harvey Kuenn, slow to pull his pitchers earlier in the Series, yanked Vuckovich at that point for lefthander Bob McClure, who had earned saves in Game Four and Game Five. For the fourth time in the Series, Herzog pulled lefthanded-hitting Ken Oberkfell for righthanded-hitting Tenace, who had gone nothing for three against McClure and had been three for 48 since late August.

But this time, Tenace — who has drawn more than 100 walks in a season several times in his career — drew another one, loading the bases. Hernandez, a former grade-school teammate of McClure in the San Francisco area, then drilled a two-run single to right center on a 3-1 pitch, tying the score.

"I was trying to protect the plate," said Hernandez. "I was vulnerable inside. I was looking fastball and I thought he might make a fat one. But he made a nasty pitch on the inside corner. I don't know how I hit it, but I did."

The next hitter, Hendrick, hit a slow chopper toward third and third baseman Molitor threw home ahead of the nose-first dive of pinch-runner Mike Ramsey, but home-plate umpire Lee Weyer ruled that the ball was foul. Hendrick then singled to right field for the go-ahead run.

Milwaukee had a righthander, Moose Haas, available to pitch to Hendrick, but Kuenn said: "They had two lefthanded hitters coming up behind George. I thought Bobby could get him out."

The Cardinals added two insurance runs in the eighth, again keyed by

Umpire Lee Weyer restrains Joaquin Andujar, the self-proclaimed "one tough Dominican," after the pitcher gets into a shouting match with the Brewers' Jim Gantner (right) in the seventh inning of Game 7 of the 1982 World Series.

a Lonnie Smith double. With Haas pitching, Hernandez was walked intentionally with one out, and Hendrick flied to center. But Porter, whose last two weeks of play erased the last two years of frustration in fans' minds, singled off lefthander Mike Caldwell, scoring Smith. Then Steve Braun, the Cardinals' third designated hitter of the game, drove in the sixth run with a single.

Braun, who rarely has batted against lefthanders in his specialist's role this season, said, "I haven't seen a lefthander since Huggins-Stengel Field at 10 o'clock in the morning." Huggins-Stengel Field in St. Petersburg, Fla., is where the Cardinals and New York Mets play 'B' games in spring training.

Andujar, pitching on a sore leg after being hit by a line drive last week, worked a scoreless seventh inning before Herzog removed him in favor of Sutter. One reason was that Herzog felt Andujar might be out of control because of a shouting match with Jim Gantner after Gantner had grounded to the mound for the last out of the inning. The hulking Weyer held Andujar back as he tried to charge Gantner.

"Joaquin sometimes gets a little high-strung in those spots," said

Cardinals fans reach to congratulate Sutter during the downtown parade to celebrate the team's World Series victory.

Herzog. "But I had told Hub (pitching coach Hub Kittle) that after the inning I was going to use Sutter, anyway.

"Once he (Andujar) got us to the seventh inning, we've got the best relief pitcher in baseball. We pay him an awful big amount of money. I figured we'd better use him."

Sutter, who had 36 saves and nine victories during the regular season and two victories and two saves in postseason play, dispatched the last six Milwaukee batters.

"Now I can say I'm just like Tug McGraw and Rollie Fingers," he said.

The reference was to two other relief aces — McGraw, here on a television assignment, was sitting to his left. Both McGraw and Fingers had been on World Series winners previously, although Fingers' inability to pitch in this Series for the Brewers gave the Cardinals a huge bullpen advantage.

Sutter does not like being called the million-dollar reliever, but he performed that way Wednesday night, as he had most of the season. "To be very honest," said Herzog, "Bruce Sutter is the guy who turned this thing around."

The Cardinals are not really champions of the world, because a large part of the world doesn't play baseball. But they are champions of the world of baseball. Nineteen eighty-two was a very good year.

COMMISH'S MOMENT

▲ Catcher Darrell Porter celebrates with reliever
Bruce Sutter after a game-ending strikeout gives
the Cardinals the 1982 World Series title.

EARLY IN THE SEASON, the "r" had been silent when the fans greeted "Bruuuce" Sutter coming out of the bullpen, but not on this night. Sutter rarely threw a straight fastball as he relied almost exclusively on his split-fingered pitch, but he fooled Gorman Thomas for the final out. Thomas had fouled off four split-fingered pitches in a row when Sutter decided, "I've got a three-run lead and nobody on, so I'm giving him a fastball."

As Darrell Porter leaped into Sutter's arms and teammates smothered them, several thousand fans jumped onto the field from the bleachers and box seats. More than 100 police officers – some on horses, some with German shepherd dogs on leashes – got the players safely off the field, then just stood by as the crowd swelled at the mound.

SEPT. 26 1983 FORSCH'S SECOND NO-HITTER

MOLLIE FORSCH SHOWED UP AT ABOUT GAME TIME at Busch Stadium, and her husband the pitcher said she wasn't a moment too soon.

"She knows how to do it," said Bob Forsch. "If she had got here late, she might not have seen me pitch."

Forsch, who spun his second career no-hitter in a 3-0 victory over the Montreal Expos, had been knocked out before the fourth inning was over on eight occasions this season. But he made a bad season a little more tasteful, becoming only the ninth pitcher in modern major league history to accomplish the following: win 20 games in a season, pitch for a World Series champion and throw two no-hitters.

The no-hitter added considerable spice to what augured to be a mundane season-closing week for the Cardinals, and it had Mollie Forsch on the edge of her seat.

"On the other no-hitter (1978), I didn't get nervous until the seventh inning," she said. "This one I started getting nervous in the fifth. The worst thing was the ninth inning. My knees were shaking and I had to stand up to see."

While Mrs. Forsch was talking to a reporter, Cardinals outfielder George Hendrick, who had not played in the game, gave her a congratulatory kiss on the cheek.

"He's been struggling," Mrs. Forsch said of her husband the pitcher. "He needed a really good game."

Forsch poured champagne afterward for all who wanted it. It may or may not have been his final victory as a Cardinal, but Manager Whitey Herzog said, "You can't give up on Forschie. He's got too much sense."

The Cardinals had talked about settling a score with Montreal catcher

Bob Forsch tips his cap to fans after pitching a no-hitter, the second of his career, against the Montreal Expos in Busch Stadium. The feat is the highlight of a season in which he struggles to a 10-12 record.

Gary Carter after some incidents last week in Montreal, and Forsch plunked Carter on the rear with a second-inning pitch. Forsch said he didn't mean anything by it, but Carter said, "He was throwing at me. I don't know why. Why don't you ask him?" Carter, however, had praise for Forsch. "He was tough. To throw a no-hitter, you've got to be tough."

Montreal manager Bill Virdon was ejected from the game along with pitcher Dan Schatzeder in the sixth inning after a pitch from Schatzeder glanced off the right arm of the Cardinals' Andy Van Slyke and then off his chin. When Forsch hit Carter, home plate umpire Harry Wendelstedt warned both benches to cease and desist.

"There's no way anybody on our team was throwing against anybody on our behalf," Virdon said. "I can't read Forsch's mind."

Wendelstedt has the distinction of umpiring in the last four no-hitters worked by Cardinals pitchers. He also was an umpire in Forsch's no-hitter here in 1978, besides working in Bob Gibson's no-hitter at Pittsurgh in 1971 and Ray Washburn's in San Francisco in 1968.

Forsch's no-hitter marked the first time a Cardinals pitcher had pitched two hitless games.

The Cardinals adhered to the superstition of not talking to Forsch about the no-hitter. "Everybody was talking, but nobody would really say anything to me," said Forsch. "I walked up to the clubhouse and the only place I heard about the no-hitter was on the radio."

The Expos' Terry Crowley, after being called out on a 2-2 pitch in the ninth inning, was ejected by Wendelstedt after an argument that might have been designed to throw Forsch off rhythm. Cardinals catcher Darrell Porter said, "When a guy's got a no-hitter, buddy, you'd better swing at that pitch."

Although Forsch is one of only 25 pitchers to throw two no-hitters, he said they were not as important as the World Series of last season. "No-hitters are nice, but all that means is that I've had two really good games," Forsch said. "The World Series means we did it for an entire season, and that feeling can't be replaced."

COMMISH'S MOMENT

FORSCH HAD BEEN BATTERED 10-1 JUST SIX DAYS BEFORE in Montreal and had given up a home run to pitcher Bill Gullickson. In the course of the game, Forsch walked Gary Carter, who yelled at Forsch to "throw strikes."

Forsch vowed to remember this when he faced the Expos again in his next start in St. Louis. On Carter's first at-bat, Forsch's control was impeccable — he hit Carter on his backside.

Long after the game was over and all the other reporters had left, I approached Forsch and he said, "Oh, I suppose you want an exclusive interview." I did, and he gave one. He also implored me to help him drink a celebratory bottle of champagne.

My notes were a little fuzzy after that.

RYNO AND WILLIE WRECK WRIGLEY

JUNE 23 1984

This is the kind of day it was at Wrigley Field . . . Willie McGee drove in six runs and became the first Cardinal to hit for the cycle since 1975, when Lou Brock did it. Yet, somebody on the other team had an even better game.

Ryne Sandberg, the Chicago Cubs' second baseman, had two home runs among five hits and drove in seven runs as the Cardinals and Cubs played one of those "you-never-know" Wrigley Field matches.

Cardinals manager Whitey Herzog, perhaps numbed by the Cubs' 11-inning victory, said, "At least those people who have the 13-run pools will be happy."

The score actually was 12-11, Cubs.

The Cardinals had the Cubs down by six runs twice and by two runs going into the bottom of the 10th inning, one strike away from victory. But Bruce Sutter, working in his fourth inning, walked Bob Dernier on a close 3-2 pitch. Then Sandberg, who had tied the game the inning before with a homer off Sutter, hit a two-run homer that tied the game again.

In the 11th, Leon Durham opened the inning by drawing a walk against lefthander Dave Rucker. Herzog, dissatisfied with Rucker's effort, immediately called on righthander Jeff Lahti, who had pitched three innings the day before.

On the hit-and-run, Durham stole second and went to third on a one-hop throw by catcher Darrell Porter that went into center field. Herzog ordered Keith Moreland and Jody Davis walked intentionally, and then Dave Owen, a spindly reserve infielder from Cleburne, Texas, lined a single to right field that drove in the winning run with nobody out.

The Cardinals, losing to the Cubs for the eighth time in 11 games, had

 Willie McGee hits for the cycle and drives in six runs but it's not enough to beat the comeback Cubs at Wrigley Field.

taken a 7-1 lead in the second inning. They took a 9-3 lead in the sixth on McGee's first homer since opening day and an 11-9 lead in the 10th on Ozzie Smith's single, his stolen base, McGee's double and two infield outs.

Sutter, in a rare off-game, couldn't hold this second lead, either. But the game had turned long before that on an admittedly brutal performance by reliever Neil Allen, who couldn't hold a 9-3 edge for rookie Ralph Citarella.

At game's end, several Cardinals sat in the dugout as if transfixed. When they moved upstairs to the clubhouse, they found teammates wearily slouched in their folding chairs, the mental fatigue having drawn even with the physical.

"I've never seen anything like this," said Cardinals third baseman Andy Van Slyke, who played less than half the game in a reserve role.

"It was like getting knocked down three times in a fight and then kay-oing the guy who had knocked you down. And they (the Cubs) were knocked down hard. Those weren't standing eight-counts."

McGee tripled home three runs in the second, an inning keyed by Citarella's first major league hit, an infield single. In the fourth, McGee singled. He hit a two-run homer to right field through the teeth of a wind in the sixth and doubled to left to put the Cardinals ahead again in the 10th.

His six RBIs represented one-third of what he had produced previously in 238 at-bats.

"He just had to be Willie McGee," said Herzog. "Stop thinking and go to swinging."

"I'm tired of thinking," said McGee. "Either you hit it or you don't."

As for Sandberg, Herzog, in an effusive moment, called him "the best player I've ever seen."

Later, he had reduced that description to best in the National League, but it was high praise, indeed.

"I don't see him doing anything wrong," said Herzog.

What Cardinals coach Red Schoendienst could appreciate about Sandberg, 24, was what Schoendienst called "his professionalism."

"After those home runs, he didn't run around the bases with his hand in the air and jumping around," said Schoendienst. "He didn't do anything. That's a professional."

Before his ninth-inning at-bat, Sandberg had been just one for 10 against Sutter in his career. One home run, let alone two, was not uppermost in his mind.

"I never dreamt that would happen," he said. "I was trying to hit the ball hard. I was looking for split-fingered fastballs. They might have started up a bit more than usual."

Sutter said he wasn't tired entering the 10th inning, despite having thrown 32 pitches in his first 2 1/3 innings. Normally, Herzog doesn't use Sutter for more than that, but he wasn't about to go without his best, either.

"I felt all right," said Sutter. "I made two bad pitches, and they both went out of the park. The guys played a great game. We just didn't hold them."

Herzog bluntly called Allen's performance "terrible," and Allen agreed.

"I'll take the brunt of the heat for this," he said. "Bruce shouldn't have had to work today. It was ridiculous what happened.

"It's just a shame to get paid that kind of money and put on a performance like that."

Allen recalled a game he had pitched here with the New York Mets a couple of years ago in which he had blown a 9-2 lead into a 10-9 defeat in two innings.

"This place," he said, "haunts the hell out of me."

COMMISH'S MOMENT

MCGEE'S CYCLE AND SIX RBIS were almost totally overlooked because of Sandberg homering twice off Sutter, the only time in his Hall of Fame career that Sutter gave up two homers to the same hitter in one game.

In Wrigley Field, the writers leave the press box in the ninth inning because they have to go through the stands to get to the clubhouses. In the case of the visiting team, they have to go through the stands and then onto the field.

Ready to write a McGee story, I found myself sitting in the third-base box seats behind an overweight gentleman who was enjoying some libations, and he loudly celebrated Sandberg's first homer in the ninth. He celebrated the second homer by losing his balance and pouring his beer over my head. "Sorry, buddy," he said.

A few moments later, upstairs in the Cardinals' clubhouse, Whitey Herzog was asked about Sandberg's performance. "He was another (expletive) Baby Ruth," Herzog said.

SEPT. 11 1985 CESAR TO THE RESCUE

NEW YORK

JOHN TUDOR IS SURE THERE WILL BE MANY GAMES that will be as important or more important for the Cardinals than this classic 1-0 victory over the New York Mets. But most assuredly this game, Tudor's ninth shutout of the season, was their most important so far.

Had Tudor not beaten the Mets, with the aid of Cesar Cedeno's 10th-inning home run, they would have fallen two games behind the Mets, who would have had momentum for a possible sweep. Instead, the teams are tied at the top in the NL East, with 25 games apiece to play.

Tudor extended his league-high streak of scoreless innings to 28 with a brilliant, three-hit effort in which no Mets player reached second base. He pitched hitless ball until Rafael Santana's single leading off the sixth. Darryl Strawberry singled to lead off the eighth, and Wally Backman threw his bat at the ball and singled behind third, leading off the 10th.

After Tudor and Dwight Gooden of the Mets had dueled to a standoff for nine innings, Cedeno, the leadoff batter in the 10th, hit an 0-2 slider from Jesse Orosco over the left-field wall. It was his 10th hit in 23 at-bats as a Cardinal and his third home run. Gooden had been lifted because Mets manager Dave Johnson felt that his total of 140 pitches was enough and keeping him in the game might be risky.

That Cedeno and Tudor should be packaged as a winning entry is a large bit of irony. The last two runs Tudor gave up, on Aug. 27 in Cincinnati, came on a pinch single by Cedeno, a hit which was his last as a Reds player. "That hit probably got me to St. Louis," he said.

This game was everything that could have been expected by a sellout crowd of 52,616. Gooden, who twice in succession has pitched nine score-

Cesar Cedeno, a late-season acquisition, jumps on home plate after hitting a 10th-inning home run that gives the Cards a victory over the Mets in a tight pennant race.

less innings and gained no decision, permitted five hits.

The Cardinals missed a good scoring chance in the eighth after Mike Jorgensen and Ozzie Smith drew bases on balls, Gooden's first two walks. But Tudor's bunt was turned into a forceout at third by first baseman Keith Hernandez.

Tudor, something of a perfectionist, chastised himself for not getting the bunt down, even though Hernandez is the league's best at making that play to third. Tudor bunted the first pitch foul and then bunted one in front of the plate, where Hernandez virtually took it off the bat.

Herzog suggested that Tudor might have done better to punch one past Hernandez, who was camped about 15 feet in front of the plate, but Tudor smiled and said, "With Dwight Gooden pitching, it was hard to watch Keith running in and try to bunt one by him, too.

"But Cesar picked me up. He's done a great job for us."

Cedeno, who has spent much of his career playing for second-division teams, is enjoying the pennant race. "I'm sure there will be a whole lot of exciting games to play, but I have to say this is one of my biggest thrills so far," Cedeno said. "I never hit a home run to tie a team for first place before."

Tudor's numbers become more remarkable every time he pitches. He leads the majors in shutouts and has three in a row. His earned-run average is 1.87. His winning streak is eight in an 18-8 season and he's won 17 of his last 18 decisions.

The lefthander insisted that he was not pitching against Gooden. "Everybody wanted to match us up," said Tudor. "Tudor against Gooden. I don't think that was fair to either one of us."

Tudor, who exhibits a seemingly implacable posture on the mound, wears the same expression off it, although he permitted himself a small gesture after striking out Darryl Strawberry to end the game. He allowed that, "I'm pretty satisfied with this game. That goes without saying."

But he added: "It was just another game for me. To be honest, I didn't take this game any differently than any others.

"I take every game in stride although I'd just as soon Dwight Gooden didn't pitch against me in this series. It turned out to be a pretty good matchup."

That large understatement aside, Tudor is looking to the final 25 games. "I'm sure there will be a lot of important games before the season is over," he said. "No one is more important than any other until you get down to the wire. This isn't the wire. We're just basically coming out of the gate."

That may be true, but the race is certainly on.

COMMISH'S MOMENT

HERZOG, CORRECTLY FEARFUL THAT SLUGGER Jack Clark would be sidelined for a long time, was looking for a righthanded extra man. That the Cardinals were able to acquire Cedeno from Cincinnati was due in large part to Herzog's friendship with former Cardinals pitcher Jim Kaat. He was the Reds' pitching coach then and conveyed to his management the Cards' interest in Cedeno. The cost was cheap — a .240-hitting outfielder at Johnson City, Tenn., named Mark Jackson, a player so obscure that Herzog admitted he never had heard of him.

The home run was the biggest September hit for Cedeno, who pulled off a blast from his Houston past and batted .434 in his only month with the Cardinals. This game probably was the most significant of the season in the Cardinals' pennant push.

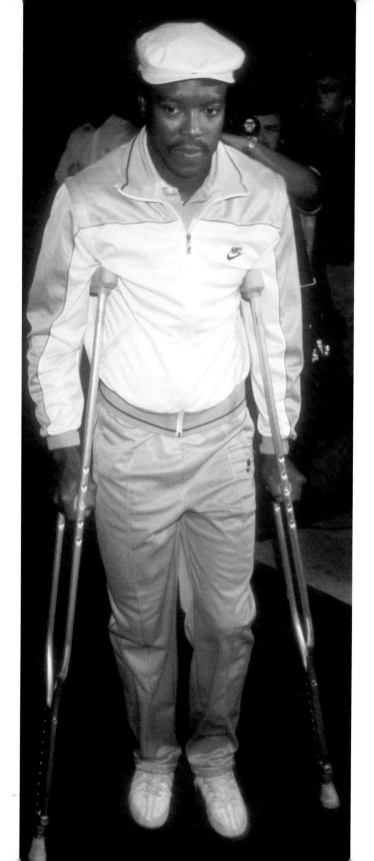

OCT. 13 1985 | TARP ATTACKS COLEMAN

CARDINALS ROOKIE OUTFIELDER VINCE COLEMAN might play again before the National League playoffs end, but he won't soon forget his brush with serious injury.

"I wouldn't wish what happened to me on my worst enemy," said Coleman, after he was pinned briefly by a runaway tarpaulin at Busch Stadium.

Coleman, who stole 110 bases in his first big-league season, apparently escaped serious injury but was unable to play in Game 4 after the stadium's slow-moving automatic tarpaulin rolled over his left leg in a bizarre pregame accident.

"It was such a freak thing," teammate Jack Clark said. "It really kind of shocked everybody. We didn't know what to do."

They recovered in championship series record fashion, scoring nine runs on eight hits in the second inning of a 12-2 victory over the Dodgers. Coleman's replacement, Tito Landrum, had four hits and drove in three runs.

According to Cardinals team surgeon Dr. Stan London, Coleman was coming off the field about two hours before game time and was going to get a bat and take batting practice in the tunnel in left field. Rain had started to fall and the automatic tarpaulin, activated by button at the right-field end of the apparatus, began rolling. According to witnesses, Coleman had just tossed his glove in the general vicinity of the dugout when the tarpaulin caught his left leg.

"He wasn't paying attention to the tarp, obviously," London said. "The tarp caught him and rolled up the outside of his leg."

One of the witnesses, Dodgers batboy Howard Hughlett, said Coleman had been looking away when the accident happened. As soon as the tarpaulin made contact, "he looked down at the ground and stepped back with his right foot," Hughlett said. "He looked like he was in an extreme

A run-in with a tarpaulin before the start of Game 4 of the National League playoffs puts speedy outfielder Vince Coleman on crutches and out of action.

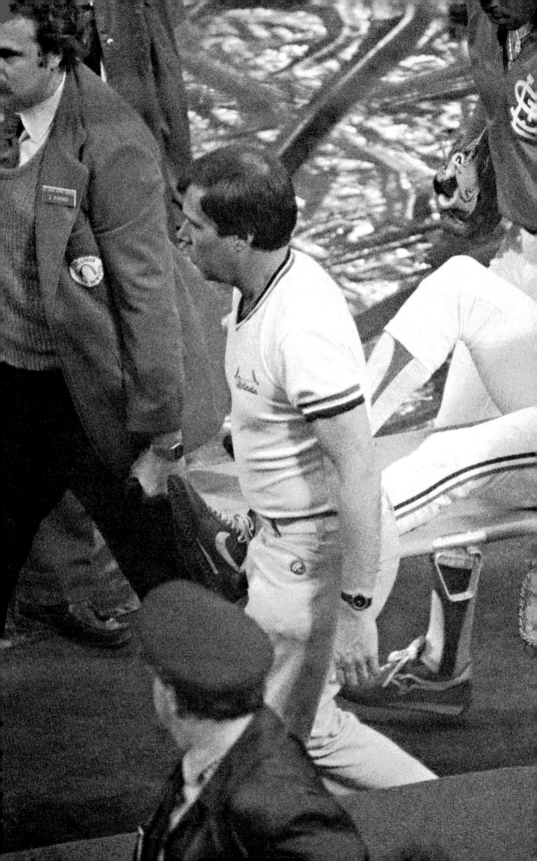

amount of pain. He was all curled up."

Hughlett said the tarp appeared to have rolled up past Coleman's hip and was on him for 10 to 15 seconds. Jim Toomey, a spokesman for the Cardinals, said the tarpaulin and cylinder weighed about 1,200 pounds together, but that weight was spread out over 180 feet. "The cylinder is made of aluminum and isn't very heavy," said Toomey. "I expect he didn't get the full impact of the 1,200 pounds."

As the tarp began rolling over his leg, Coleman screamed in blood-curdling fashion. He said it was from fear and pain.

Replaying his anxious moments for the press, Coleman said, "My shoe got caught in the tarp. I tried to get it loose and it continued to grab me. It went right up to my thigh. There I was with 1,500 pounds of tarp on my leg. Thank God the grounds-crew person managed to shut it off when he did.

"The worst part of it was they had to roll the tarp back over my leg."

Coleman apparently was pulled free by several members of the Cardinals, and Toomey said, "Coleman probably was not as severely hurt because of the quick action of the grounds crew member operating the machine."

Cardinals players, police and security tried to keep photographers and writers away from Coleman as he lay on the turf. When the outfielder was carried off the field on a stretcher, people were pushing and shoving and making threats. No one was seriously hurt.

After Coleman was injured, Cardinals manager Whitey Herzog called the rookie speedster's mother in Jacksonville, Fla., and assured her that Coleman was all right. Mrs. Coleman called back later and asked, "Are you sure I don't need to come up there?"

Herzog replied, "No. We've got Willie and Ozzie to mother him," referring to Coleman's friends, Willie McGee and Ozzie Smith.

Terry Pendleton (9) helps trainer Gene Gieselmann (left) and other Cardinals personnel carry Coleman off the field on a stretcher.

▲ After the automatic tarp puts a wet blanket on the Cards' postseason hopes by taking down Coleman, the grounds crew manually removes the smaller tarps covering the bases.

COMMISH'S MOMENT

THE CARDINALS DIDN'T FEEL THE LOSS of Coleman right away. In fact, they finished off the Dodgers with three wins in a row and won the first two games of the I-70 World Series in Kansas City.

But, in the long run, they certainly felt Coleman's absence as they lost to an inferior Royals team. A tiny bone chip on the outside of his knee, where the tarp had rolled up his leg, made it too painful for Coleman to play. With Willie McGee uncomfortable in the leadoff spot, the Cardinals stole just two bases and scored only 13 runs in seven games while batting .185.

OCT. 14 1985 — OZZIE'S 'GO CRAZY' HOME RUN

CALL IT A 3,000-TO-1 SHOT. That's how many times Ozzie Smith had batted lefthanded in the major leagues - actually 3,009 - without hitting a home run. He hadn't even hit one in Walla Walla, where he played Class A ball.

But that longshot broke the tape for the Cardinals in the ninth inning of Monday's fifth game of the National League Championship Series with the Los Angeles Dodgers. Smith drilled a 1-2 pitch from Tom Niedenfuer off a concrete pillar behind the right-field wall at Busch Stadium and the Cardinals had a 3-2 victory and a 3-2 lead in the best-of-seven series.

Before Monday, Smith had 13 home runs in his major-league career — all from his natural right side. And those home runs covered eight seasons as a major leaguer.

"That's not really what I was trying to do," Smith said. "I was trying to get an extra-base hit and get into scoring position. Fortunately, I was able to get the ball up."

The home run created a mob scene at the plate as Smith high-fived his way home.

"The timing of that," teammate Jack Clark said, "was spectacular. It's something a player dreams about. It's something a guy works 162 games for. It's something he'll never forget; it's something we'll never forget.

"All the right buttons were pushed on that one."

Smith had his best offensive season this year with a .276 average, 6 homers and 53 runs batted in. "The little midget," as pitcher Joaquin Andujar colorfully refers to him, "is a strong little guy. He's stronger than people think."

Dodgers manager Tom Lasorda took out starter Fernando Valenzuela in the ninth inning and Niedenfuer, who had stopped the Cardinals in the first game, came in. Niedenfuer, like almost everyone else, was surprised at the result.

 Ozzie Smith hits one of the most memorable homers in Busch Stadium history, driving a Tom Niedenfuer fastball for a game-winning homer in the NL playoffs.

▲ Cardinals fans heed broadcaster Jack Buck's cry to "Go crazy, folks!" as Smith circles the bases after hitting his game-winning drive.

"I thought it would be on the warning track," he said of Smith's drive. "It's just one of those things. I have to put it out of my mind and look ahead to the future. Let's give Ozzie some credit, too. He's really improved left-handed and he got around on my fastball today."

Lasorda was more expansive.

"Naturally," Lasorda said, "I'm dumbstruck. In all my years in baseball, you learn one thing — never expect the expected to happen. If Ozzie had 25 or 30 home runs, you could understand it. But this is what makes baseball so great."

By Smith's admission, "That's not really what I expect to do when I'm hitting lefthanded. I'm 150 pounds. I wasn't born to be 6-1 or 6-2. Home runs aren't my thing. I was born to hit the ball in the gap."

The Cardinals stranded 10 men before Smith put a stunning end to the 2-2 tie.

"I've felt all along," he said, "that I was a much better offensive player than I was given credit for. Just because I didn't have a high average, people were thinking I couldn't hit. This year I did hit for a high average."

The $2 million man obviously can do more than catch grounders and do handsprings.

"People have always talked about how important defense is," said Smith. "In any sport, like basketball, defense puts you into position to win. I feel I do as well at what I do as any offensive player does, so why shouldn't I get paid as much?"

Would it be too much to suggest that there was a therapeutic effect to Smith's home run besides the obvious?

Just minutes after the game, injured outfielder Vince Coleman, who had arrived at the park on crutches, was walking away from the clubhouse under his own power. "I threw them away," said Coleman.

▼ Niedenfuer heads for the showers as Smith, trailed by coach Hal Lanier, heads for home plate and the victory celebration.

COMMISH'S MOMENT

FOR JUST A MOMENT, I STOOD IN THE PRESS BOX and wondered if the ball Ozzie hit was still in play. Dodgers right fielder Mike Marshall quickly got the ball off the back wall and fired it to the infield.

But when Ozzie fired his fist into the air between second and third, and when Dodgers shortstop Mariano Duncan didn't attempt to tag Smith, you knew the game was over.

Ironically, Smith and Niedenfuer almost collided as the pitcher trudged off the mound and the batter hopped and skipped — sort of his own "Go crazy!" moment — between third and home.

Slugger Jack Clark carries Smith off the field after the homer hero is mobbed by teammates at home plate.

OCT. 16 1985 CLARK'S CLINCHER

LOS ANGELES

IT WAS FOR A MOMENT SUCH AS THIS that Jack Clark was acquired last winter by the Cardinals from the San Francisco Giants.

Runners at second and third, two outs, Cardinals trailing the Los Angeles Dodgers by one run in the ninth inning of a playoff game that would enable the Dodgers to tie the series at three games apiece if they won.

Dodgers manager Tom Lasorda surprisingly eschewed an intentional walk. Clark then swung at Tom Niedenfuer's first pitch, threw down his bat, looked triumphantly into the Cardinals dugout and slowly began the happiest base-circling of his career. He never watched the flight of the ball.

"The only thing I saw was the ball looking like a laser beam. It was serious Star Wars," said on-deck hitter Andy Van Slyke.

Clark's three-run drive landed halfway up the pavilion section in left field and gave the Cardinals a 7-5 victory and passage to the World Series against Kansas City. After losing the first two games of the series to the Dodgers, the Cardinals won the last four. This will be the first post-season matchup of Missouri's baseball teams, both of which the Cardinals' Whitey Herzog has managed.

"That ball would have had to hit the (Goodyear) blimp and come straight down to stay in this ball park," Niedenfuer said of Clark's home run. "That must have been at least 500 feet."

On Clark's previous at-bat, after the Cardinals had tied the score with a three-run rally in the seventh, Clark had struck out on Niedenfuer sliders. "I tried to slip a fastball by him," said Niedenfuer of the second encounter. "I can honestly say I got beat with my best pitch."

But Clark is a hitter who says he looks only for fastballs. "All day

Jack Clark gets a rowdy reception after hitting the ninth-inning home run that won the NL playoffs for the Cardinals.

Joaquin Andujar gives fellow pitcher John Tudor a champagne dousing during the Cardinals' pennant-victory celebration.

long I really hadn't had a good swing," he said. "I made a slight adjustment in my stance the last time up. I was pretty close to the plate and I took a half-step back. It just was enough to square me up a little bit more."

Of the homer and his look to the dugout, Clark said, "I knew it was going to be a home run. That was for my teammates. I'm not the hero or the reason why we're here. It was special for me but more special for them."

Clark continued, "I was looking for a fastball, but I was just looking for a basehit to tie the score. That's usually when I get my home runs, when I'm trying for basehits."

The Dodgers went ahead 5-4 in the eighth when Mike Marshall's fly ball to right got up in the jetstream and went over Van Slyke's jump for a home run. "It got up in the Sandinista winds," said Van Slyke, who meant to say Santa Ana winds. "I didn't think it was going to go out. I just missed it by a couple of inches."

In the Cardinals' ninth, Cesar Cedeno struck out but Willie McGee battled from a 0-2 count and hit a single, his third of the game. "I think I'm a better two-strike hitter," said McGee, "than I am when the count is 0-0. I think I concentrate better when I have two strikes."

Then, running on his own, McGee stole second. He had been thrown out by Mike Scioscia once before in the game but he said, "We can't stop, especially in a situation like that. You've got to make them throw you out."

Ozzie Smith, named the series' Most Valuable Player by acclamation, coaxed a walk. Tom Herr grounded out, setting it up for Clark, or if Lasorda chose, Van Slyke.

Lasorda chose to allow Niedenfuer to pitch to Clark rather than have a lefthander, Jerry Reuss, face Van Slyke or Brian Harper, who would have pinch hit for Van Slyke. "If I had a lefthanded pitcher, it might have been a different story," said Lasorda, tartly.

Lasorda told the media, "I wanted the righthander against the righthander. He had struck him out the other time up and the shadows were coming in.

"And I didn't want the bases loaded where he couldn't make a pitch, where if he walks a guy the game is tied."

Privately, a tearful Lasorda told his players, "It was my fault. I should have walked Clark.

"This is one of the worst losses I've ever had to experience," said Lasorda.

Van Slyke said, "I was looking for Tommy Lasorda to put four fingers up. You can't second-guess Tommy Lasorda. He made all the right moves . . . but he got burned."

Herzog diplomatically said, "I always try to manage both clubs. I thought possibly he would (walk Clark). He went strength against strength. He had one choice and he made a choice. It turned out wrong. If you guys would have told him not to pitch to Clark . . . but none of you went down there."

Clark missed 37 games in the last two months of the season with a strained muscle in his left side, an injury he had twice. "Because of the injury I had, I was compensating in my swing, trying to protect my side," Clark said. "It took a while to get turned around. It was just a matter of time before I hit one."

Clark hit his first home run since Sept. 21 and only his second since Aug. 16. "All I was trying to do was just take three good swings," said Clark. "I've been in that situation before. It was time for some type of results.

"That was the greatest one of my career," he said.

Cesar Cedeno puts a bottle of bubbly to good use on manager Whitey Herzog.

COMMISH'S MOMENT

RARELY DOES A MANAGER ALLOW A RELIEVER to face the other team's slugger twice in a game, but Dodgers manager Tommy Lasorda did just that with Game 6 loser Tom Niedenfuer.

Almost unbelievably in the seventh, Lasorda walked Tom Herr intentionally to let Niedenfuer get to Jack Clark, who struck out with runners at first and third and one out in a tie game.

In the ninth, Lasorda had lefthander Jerry Reuss warmed up to face lefthanded-hitting Andy Van Slyke, if Lasorda chose to walk Clark then. Since Van Slyke did so poorly against lefthanders that year, Cardinals manager Whitey Herzog probably would have pinch hit righthanded-hitting Brian Harper.

But Lasorda let Niedenfuer pitch to Clark again, with a one-run lead and two Cardinals on base. As the ball rocketed over left fielder Pedro Guerrero's head, he probably spoke for baffled Dodgers fans everywhere when he slammed his mitt to the ground.

◀ **Die-hard fans lie in wait for World Series tickets to go on sale at Busch Stadium after the Cardinals win the pennant.**

Pitcher Todd Worrell takes the throw as Kansas City's Jorge Orta is ruled safe in what umpire Don Denkinger calls a "bang-bang play" in Game 6 of the 1985 World Series. TV replays show the throw easily beat Orta.

OCT. 26 1985 DENKINGER'S BLOWN CALL

FOR KANSAS CITY'S DANE IORG, the ninth inning of Game Six of the World Series was a "dream." For Cardinals manager Whitey Herzog, it was a bitter nightmare.

The Cardinals were two outs away from a world championship before former Cardinal Iorg, a hero of their 1982 championship team, delivered a two-run, bases-loaded pinch single in the bottom of the ninth to give the Kansas City Royals a 2-1 victory and prolong the World Series and the state championship to a seventh game.

Brian Harper had given the Cardinals a 1-0 lead in the eighth with a two-out pinch single off Kansas City starter Charlie Leibrandt. But the Cardinals' defense buckled in the ninth and, more importantly, they were hurt by a close call at first base as they lost a game they led after eight innings for the first time in 89 such situations this season.

The bottom of the ninth began with Darryl Motley batting for Pat Sheridan and Herzog relieving with Todd Worrell for Ken Dayley. Kansas City countered with lefthanded-hitting Jorge Orta, who hit a chopper to the right side. First baseman Jack Clark, second baseman Tom Herr and Worrell all headed that way, with Clark making the grab. He took a couple of steps before throwing on the run to Worrell at first base, but the throw still appeared to beat Orta easily.

Umpire Don Denkinger, despite heated protests by the Cardinals, ruled that Orta was safe. "He said he beat the throw," said Herzog. "I said, 'How could he, if he stepped on Worrell's foot?'"

Worrell confirmed that Orta "came down on the back of my foot, which was on the bag, after I had the ball in my glove. When Whitey was arguing with him, (Denkinger) said my foot was up off the top of the bag when I caught the ball.

"I don't know how I can have my foot in the air and still have somebody step on it."

In television replays that will leave an indelible imprint on St. Louis

▲ Second baseman Tom Herr protests the call to Denkinger, who tells manager Whitey Herzog, "I did the best I could."

baseball lore if the Cardinals lose Game Seven, Orta was shown to be out.

Denkinger said, "It was a bang-bang play. The throw was high. In my judgment the runner was on first before the catch and I called him safe. ... I did the best I could. Whitey said to me, 'We can't catch a break,' and I said, 'That's the way I saw it.' "

Said Herzog, "We had the damned World Series won tonight."

Steve Balboni, the next hitter after Orta, lofted a foul near the television camera at the first-base dugout. Clark and catcher Darrell Porter appeared confused as to who would get the ball, which ultimately dropped behind Clark.

A reprieved Balboni, previously a bust in postseason play, grounded a single to left. Jim Sundberg bunted and Worrell threw to third to get the slow-footed Orta, who strangely had been allowed to run for himself.

But on a 1-0 pitch to pinch-hitter Hal McRae, Porter swatted at and missed a Worrell slider and was charged with a passed ball, moving runners to second and third. Herzog set up a double-play situation by intentionally walking McRae.

Iorg, who set a designated hitter's record when he went 9 for 17 in the 1982 Series, batted for Dan Quisenberry. Herzog had lefthander Rick Horton ready.

But, perhaps figuring the Royals would go to righthanded-hitting Lynn Jones (2 for 2 in the Series), he left the hard-throwing Worrell in, even though Iorg has had much more experience than Jones as a pinch-hitter.

"I got jammed and he broke my bat," said Iorg of his game-winner. "But as soon as I hit it, I knew it was a base hit." Iorg displayed for a reporter a bat with a crack on the bottom half. "This is going in the trophy case," he said.

"These are the situations you dream about as a child," he said. "I've dreamed about that situation many times. To be here, to fulfill that dream, is very special."

Iorg said that there was nothing special, though, about having that hit against the Cardinals, who sold him to Kansas City for a modest $30,000 in 1984. "It was an important enough at-bat," said Iorg, "without thinking about the past and who it was against.

"I wasn't nervous. I've pinch-hit for many years in a lot of situations. I know this was the most important, but I know how to react in that situation."

Leibrandt pitched five perfect innings for the Royals and had given up only sixth-inning bloop hits to Cesar Cedeno and Porter before the eighth. "We faced another Lefty Grove," said Herzog, whose team is batting a dismal .190 for the Series.

With one out in the St. Louis eighth, Terry Pendleton guided a single to right field past first baseman Balboni, who was guarding the foul line to protect against an extra-base hit. Cedeno then walked on a 3-2 pitch. Porter was called out on strikes before Harper, hitless since Sept. 3 — his last 14 at-bats — broke his bat on a single to center, scoring Pendleton.

"It's very strange to go from celebration to mourning," Harper said. "Now we have to keep it on an even profile."

Steaming about the ninth-inning call, Herzog tried to restrain himself but couldn't. "We've got no more chance of winning (Game Seven) than a man in the moon because that guy is behind the plate," Herzog said of Denkinger.

"As long as you don't get the best umpires in the World Series, you've got to put up with that stuff. The only thing I know is the best teams are in the World Series. We should have the best umpires in the World Series, too. Let the other guys watch on TV. Maybe they'll learn something.

"I think it's a disgrace. The whole inning got messed up when he missed that call at first base. Dane didn't exactly murder the ball. But the whole inning was messed up."

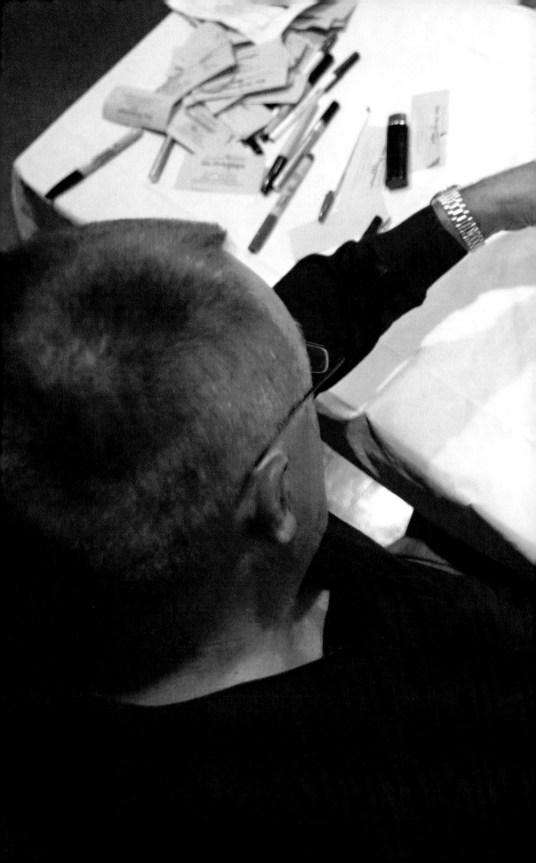

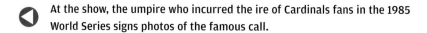
Denkinger, now retired, comes to St. Louis in 2004 for a memorabilia show.

At the show, the umpire who incurred the ire of Cardinals fans in the 1985 World Series signs photos of the famous call.

COMMISH'S MOMENT

ONE OF THE KEY PLAYS IN THE FATEFUL NINTH INNING came when catcher Darrell Porter committed a passed ball on a Todd Worrell slider, prompting Manager Whitey Herzog to intentionally walk veteran Hal McRae and load the bases. Pinch-hitter Dane Iorg followed with the two-run single that ended the game.

It wasn't until spring training the next season that Worrell told me that he had seen Porter go to his mask — apparently accidentally — and Worrell thought it meant changing the sign between fastball and slider.

Porter, who did not react to the pitch, may have just been scratching his nose. But Worrell, who had been in the majors only two months, was afraid to call time to ask Porter, assuming the veteran knew what he was doing.

Players end up in a variety of poses when a fight erupts in a game between the Cardinals and the San Francisco Giants after Vince Coleman gets hit by a pitch.

JULY 23 1986 WHITEY BRAWL

THERE WERE 27 HITS IN THE CARDINALS' 10-7 VICTORY over the San Francisco Giants, but there were many more fireworks in a seventh-inning brawl that involved players, managers and coaches from both teams for 15 minutes of extracurricular activity.

Two Giants players and manager Roger Craig were ejected from the game, and Cardinals second baseman Tom Herr suffered an eight-stitch gash near his left ear when he tried to break up a scuffle.

The flame for the fight was the Giants' indignance over Vince Coleman stealing second and third with the Cardinals ahead 10-2 in the fifth inning. Coleman eventually was out at home on a tag play as he tried to score on a Juan Berenguer pitch that hit the backstop, and when Berenguer made the tag, he spiked the ball. Both benches erupted after Berenguer yelled at Coleman and Coleman tipped his helmet, but there was no fighting — this time.

When Coleman came to bat in the seventh, Frank Williams threw one pitch close to Coleman, and umpire Bob Davidson issued a warning to both benches. The next pitch hit Coleman, prompting the automatic ejection of Williams and Craig.

When those ejections were made, San Francisco third baseman Chris Brown became upset and had to be restrained. Both benches emptied, and the melee was on. San Francisco pitcher Mike Krukow took a bull rush at Coleman, and Coleman tackled him.

Players still were milling around and the umpires almost had it broken up when Cardinals manager Whitey Herzog and Craig began jawing. Craig and Herzog got shoves in as umpire John McSherry tried to restrain them, and then the momentum of all the players carried them into a large pile-up near the screen.

"(Bleep) Roger Craig," Herzog said of Craig's criticism of the Cards' running game. "What the hell. Our club can't score. They've got the tying runs at the plate (in the ninth). I guess he thinks he invented the damn game or something. I can't believe this game. He started the whole thing.

"(Craig) told Williams to hit Vince. We're not supposed to run in the fifth? I wish he'd send me a note over and say they're not going to score 10 runs."

Herzog said that when he and Craig were nose-to-nose in the argument, Craig told Herzog to stop running. "I told him, 'We're not going to stop it. We're going to run in the fifth inning. I can tell you that right now.'

"Evidently he thinks it's wrong. I'll tell him right now. I'll never stop running now against that sucker."

Herzog and Cardinals pitcher Rick Horton were involved in a double-team with Joel Youngblood of the Giants — Herzog threw Youngblood to the ground — after Cardinals pitching coach Mike Roarke had fallen to the ground, either a victim of a Jeff Leonard blow or, as Roarke said, by tripping over Leonard's leg.

Herzog then went for a clothesline on San Francisco's Randy Kutcher, and Kutcher threw him off. "Well," said Herzog, laughing, "it was fun."

But there was no question that Herzog and Craig have different philosophies about the running game, and it really was no laughing matter.

Craig said: "Letting him steal with an eight-run lead — if that's his game plan, he's going to have a few more fights. I thought it was bush. I respect him as a manager and a friend, but that's bull.

"Whitey said, 'I didn't tell him to run.' I said, 'Hell, you're in control of him, aren't you?' "

Herzog said he had, indeed, given Coleman a green light. "He's on his own in the fifth inning," he said.

Craig said: "I'm glad it happened. It woke my ballclub up. We'll whip their butts after what happened tonight."

The Giants' Bob Brenly didn't approve of Coleman's actions. "If you'd talked to me about an hour ago, I'd have given you a whole bookful of quotes about what a low-rent sucker Vince Coleman is."

Brenly continued: "It's an unwritten baseball law. They were kicking the snot out of us. There was no need to rub it in. I feel he was trying to show us up."

Coleman said he used his football background to tackle Krukow. "I got him around the legs. I did just what they told me when I was a little boy. I was like a defensive back."

The Cardinals' outfielder said he was not surprised at what happened after the steals. "When I was on third base, everybody was hollering at me.

Herzog's brash, bare-knuckle style makes him a favorite of Cardinals fans.

To be honest, after they gave the warning, I didn't think they'd throw at me again."

Coleman said: "I wasn't there to show anybody up. I have a goal that I'm trying to attain — to break the record (130 steals). Whitey gave me the green light to go.

"I could see if it was Curt Ford or Jose Oquendo trying to steal bases to try to show somebody up. When you say Vince Coleman, he's a base stealer."

Kutcher, who had the Cardinals' Oquendo under his left arm before Herzog attempted a clothesline, said: "All I'm trying to do is break things up. And Whitey says, 'Oh, you want some of me?' I just got up here (to the majors). I'm not going after anybody, and I wouldn't go after that guy."

Herzog was cheered wildly by the Busch Stadium fans, who chanted, "WHITE-EE, WHITE-EE."

COMMISH'S MOMENT

WE CAUGHT A QUICK GLIMPSE OF A LARGE MAN in street clothes on the field during the brawl, and it turned out to be Cardinals pitcher Danny Cox — never one to duck a confrontation.

Cox had been charting pitches behind the screen when he decided he should lend assistance. Home-plate umpire Bob Davidson shooed him away, telling Cox if the other fans saw someone in street clothes on the field, they might think it's another fan and decide to jump in, too.

So Cox ran to the Cardinals clubhouse, put on his uniform and ran back to the field. Davidson didn't stop him this time.

AUG. 5 1986 OZZIE'S GREATEST CATCH

OZZIE SMITH DRESSED HURRIEDLY so that he could go home and watch television. Even he wanted to see this one.

In the Ozzie Smith Video of Death-Defying Catches and Other Mind-Boggling Plays, the one he made in the ninth inning off Philadelphia's Von Hayes will merit watching more than once.

With a man at first and one out, Smith, running with his back to the infield, left his feet in an attempt to snare Hayes' popup. He avoided left fielder Curt Ford, who dived at the same time, and retained the ball in snow-cone fashion in his glove after gravity took over.

With a crowd of more than 27,000 at Busch Stadium provoked into a frenzy, the Cardinals won 3-2 in the bottom of the ninth when Smith dashed home to score the winning run on Terry Pendleton's one-out squeeze bunt with the bases loaded.

Abetted by Vince Coleman's four stolen bases, this game had more than its share of entertainment for two teams that collectively are about 40 games out of first place.

"Our fans have been good around here all year," Smith said. "Obviously, the team hasn't played the way we're capable, but we haven't stopped giving it our all. It may not look like it, but we give it our all every day."

With the game tied 2-2 in the ninth, Mike Schmidt beat out an infield hit to deep short against Todd Worrell. Glenn Wilson struck out and then Hayes, pinch-hitting for Rick Schu, lofted a blooper to short left-center field.

Ford, who was playing deep, charged in. Smith, who was playing in his normal position, charged out. Smith takes over the commentary:

"All I'm trying to do is get to the spot where I think the ball is going to come down," he said. "When I looked out and I saw that Curt was probably not going to get there, then I figured I was probably going to have to dive. I'm just going to dive where I think the ball would come down.

 Ozzie Smith's backflips are a featured attraction at Busch Stadium in the 1980s.

"It was a matter of us both diving at the same time and hopefully not both diving the same way.

"I guess that's the first one in a while that everybody got excited about. It was a pretty good one. I didn't see it. Maybe I can catch it on the news."

Although Smith wasn't sure where this catch would rank on the hit parade, others weren't hesitant.

"Best play I've ever seen," Cardinals announcer Mike Shannon said.

"It might have been the best catch I've ever seen," Phillies manager John Felske said. "It's hard to imagine a better one than that. If the ball falls, with them both on the ground, it might have rolled to the wall."

Coleman: "Only one player who can make that play."

Worrell: "He wasn't even lined up on that one. He dove and saw the ball come over his shoulder."

For Ford, it was the best catch he never saw.

"When I saw he was coming as hard as he could, I thought I'd better get down. After that, I didn't see it."

What happened was that Ford virtually dived under Smith. Almost miraculously, there was no contact.

Smith made a routine — for him — backpedaling catch of John Russell's popup to end the inning and then Coleman started the Cardinals' ninth with a double.

Given the green light by manager Whitey Herzog, Coleman stole third, inducing the Phillies to walk Smith and Tom Herr intentionally. Ford's grounder forced Coleman at home, and Pendleton was next, riding a 10-game hitting streak. "I kind of figured I'd get a chance to swing the bat," he said.

But Herzog thought that a squeeze was a safer bet. "We need three outs to drive in a run," he said. "If he pops it up, we look like a bunch of dummies."

Pendleton pushed the ball toward first base. Hayes barehanded the ball and threw desperately toward the plate. But catcher Russell could not make connections as Smith scored, and Cardinals streamed in high-five fashion from the dugout as if they were 1 1/2 games out of first rather than 21 1/2.

"If I was a paying fan," Coleman said, "tonight I got my money's worth."

Ozzie Smith glides over a baserunner on the way to one of his 13 consecutive Gold Gloves.

COMMISH'S MOMENT

THE BRILLIANCE OF OZZIE SMITH'S CATCH, which preserved a tie score until the Cardinals won it with a squeeze bunt in the bottom of the ninth, disguised a typical lineup of this lost season.

With five-game winner Tim Conroy on the mound, the Cardinals hardly could have had a more punchless batting order than that which featured Curt Ford batting fourth and Mike LaValliere, Clint Hurdle and Tito Landrum batting sixth through eighth.

Hurdle came in batting .195, Landrum .210 and LaValliere .234. And cleanup man Ford? He hit two homers in 1986. In Whitey Herzog's world, they didn't even qualify as "Punch-and-Judy" hitters — he often referred to his batting order as "a bunch of Judies."

APRIL 18 1987 SEAT CUSHION SLAM

IT WAS OCTOBER IN APRIL on Saturday night at Busch Stadium.

In one of the most bizarre, dramatic baseball games this early in the season, Tom Herr's first career grand slam gave the Cardinals a 12-8 victory over the defending World Series champion New York Mets in 10 innings.

Fans sent thousands of souvenirs from Seat Cushion Night sailing onto the field, and drivers honked horns in the streets and parking garages as though the Cardinals had won their 100th game rather than their sixth.

Herr, whose double had helped the Cardinals erase the Mets' early 5-0 lead, connected against Jesse Orosco after rookie Tom Pagnozzi had tied the game with his first big-league hit earlier in the inning. Herr drove in six runs.

"I knew it was out when I hit it," Herr said. "It was a great feeling seeing everybody waiting at home plate and going a little crazy."

From Orosco's standpoint, the first-pitch fastball prompted him to say, "Oh, no."

"I was hoping it would hit a bird or something," he said.

For Herr, the moment ranked in "the top five" of his career.

"If it had been in October, it would have been a little higher," he said. "Maybe down the road you can look back and say this was a big win for us and a big loss for them. But I would be very surprised if this fazed them a whole lot."

This was a full-moon game from the very beginning.

"I don't know if it was very entertaining," Cardinals manager Whitey Herzog said. "I guess that will be the end of seat cushion day."

Among other strange happenings Saturday night . . .

A foul ball — on a squeeze bunt attempt — was kicked into the Cardinals' dugout by the Mets' Keith Hernandez, who was surprised to see it come flying back out in his direction.

The Cardinals' Terry Pendleton had taken umbrage with Hernandez's act, but

 Members of the Busch Stadium grounds crew collect seat cushions that are thrown onto the field after the Cardinals rally from a 5-0 deficit against the Mets. The cushions had been given to fans as part of a promotion.

Hernandez said the men made their peace later in the game at first base.

"It was two competitors," Hernandez said. "It was the heat of the battle.

"I shouldn't have kicked the ball in the dugout. I was wrong. It was like a Jan Stenerud field goal."

When Herr's double put the Cardinals ahead 6-5 in the sixth, hundreds of seat cushions rained onto the field, causing a delay of six minutes.

The Cardinals, not known for their come-from-behind antics last year, relinquished the lead in the ninth, tied the game in the bottom of the ninth, fell behind in the 10th, then tied it again in the bottom of the 10th when Pagnozzi got his first hit following singles by Pendleton and Steve Lake. Ozzie Smith walked to load the bases for Herr, who crushed a drive over the left-field wall.

Within minutes, seat cushions blanketed the playing surface.

Danny Cox, the Cardinals' starter who was knocked out after three innings, said, "It was one of the most exciting games I've ever watched. I wish I would've played in it."

First base draws the attention of Ozzie Smith (left) and
Tom Herr, as well as the Mets' Keith Hernandez, after
Herr's throw completes a double play. The game ends
when Herr hits a grand slam in the 10th inning.

COMMISH'S MOMENT

AS PREDICTED BY WHITEY HERZOG, it was the last Seat Cushion Night in this ball-park as it took the Busch Stadium crew virtually all night to get the field ready for the Sunday afternoon game.

All the commotion stemmed from the first of just two homers Tom Herr would hit all sea-son, even though he drove in 83 runs. Back in the clubhouse, an usher who had retrieved the home-run ball presented it to Herr, who asked, "Is it dented on the side?"

The victory was particularly pleasing to the Cardinals because the "Pond Scum" Mets had swept them in four April games in St. Louis the year before, then proceeded to bury the Cardinals and everybody else as they raced off to their second world championship.

OCT. 1 1987 'GO HOME METS!'

THERE IS NO NEED for scoreboard updates, no more magic numbers.

Danny Cox, the Cardinals' version of Mr. October, and veteran Dan Driessen, who has had past autumnal glories, led the Cardinals to their third National League Eastern Division title in six seasons with an 8-2 victory over the Montreal Expos.

"It's a miracle," said manager Whitey Herzog. "It's the Miracle of 250 Stadium Plaza."

The Cardinals have been in first place since May 20 — 134 days — but they spent the better part of the summer fighting off the advances of the Expos and New York Mets. At their high point, the Cardinals led by 9 1/2 games and at their lowest by 1 1/2.

Then they tried to hang on without slugger Jack Clark, who has been out 21 games, and Willie McGee, who missed the clinching game.

After allowing a tainted run in the first inning, Cox retired 16 batters in succession before allowing the Expos' second hit. He gave up only five hits, including a home run by Tim Wallach in the ninth.

Driessen, the offensive and defensive star of the game, drove in two runs with a double in the fourth inning. A former standout with Cincinnati's "Big Red Machine," Driessen was a late-season call-up from Louisville.

"He really played a game," Herzog said. "He's played some good ball-games for us and then he's had some tough times. The last three or four games, he's struggled, but he rose to the occasion tonight. He kind of inspired everybody."

Driessen made diving stops at first base in the sixth and seventh innings. At 10:15 p.m., Cox fired to Driessen for the final out, sending a crowd of 52,864 into an Adult T-Shirt Night-waving frenzy, chanting, "Go home, Mets!" Among the spectators were a few members of the Mets, who

Danny Cox has ample reason to smile after pitching the Cardinals to a division-clinching victory over the Montreal Expos.

▲ **Members of the Mets, including mustachioed ex-Cardinal Keith Hernandez (center), are on hand for the Cards' clincher.**

already were in town for a season-ending series at Busch.

"I don't worry about who's watching the game," Cox said. "Three million fans are coming through these gates this year. (The Mets) are probably the only ones who didn't enjoy what they saw."

The Cardinals exploded onto the field for the celebration, led by Tom Herr. The normally reserved infielder ripped off his uniform shirt and began waving it wildly to the crowd. He exited by blowing kisses to the fans.

Cox won just one of six decisions in September and had won only two games since July 4, but he put a summer of discontent behind him with one of his strongest efforts of the season.

"Hell, yes, I wanted to complete the game," Cox said. "I haven't done it all year. I wanted to show them I could still do it.

"This is my biggest game. This is what it's all about. I've always dreamed about pitching the game when you win it all. Tonight was a dream come true."

The Cardinals overcame a seeming inordinate number of injuries to win the division title. John Tudor and Tony Pena both went out in April.

Clark has been out — with the exception of one pinch-hit at-bat — since Sept. 9.

"You don't hear about all our injuries," Herzog said. "We've played 159 games and I venture to say we had our starting lineup out there about 25 times.

"The fact that we won with Jack sitting out 21 games . . . I think that says something."

McGee, a part of his third division championship, said, "It's just beautiful to sit here and be able to drink a bottle of champagne."

There were 12 cases of Jacques Bonet champagne, ordered by equipment manager Buddy Bates. Some of it was drunk. Most of it was worn, as were cups of the owner's product.

McGee, continuing to revel in the moment, said all the championships had "special meaning but this one was the toughest because we struggled so much the second half. But we held on to what he had."

Since the Cardinals reached their high-water mark of 61-32, they have won 33 and lost 33. Without Clark, after his most recent injury, they are 13-8.

Although they didn't prosper without Clark, they endured.

"People were always saying we were about to be overtaken, but it never happened," third baseman Terry Pendleton said.

Proud club president Gussie Busch said, "I've never got a greater kick out of anything than I did tonight, coming in here and winning as easy as we did."

Then, he turned to Herzog and said, "God bless you. Let's do it again."

Herzog raised an eyebrow in mock protest. He said, "Hey, wait a minute. When I came here, you said, 'One more time.' "

Players erupt from the dugout to celebrate with their teammates on the field after beating the Expos.

▲ Pennant-clincher euphoria prompts fans to celebrate in various ways, including handstands.

◀ Pitcher Joe Magrane gives outfielder Vince Coleman a beer bath during the celebration.

COMMISH'S MOMENT

A DOZEN OR SO METS, including former Cardinal first baseman Keith Hernandez, sat in press-level boxes at Busch, hoping against hope that Montreal would win the finale of a four-game series and give the Mets at least a chance to tie for the title.

Fans hurled insults like, "Hernandez, you're a bum. Go back to New York!" But he would just smile and raise his glass, as if to toast them as champions.

While Danny Cox's complete game was the clincher, the Cardinals probably won the division crown two days before that. Lefthanded rookie Joe Magrane blanked the Expos 1-0 in the first game of a twi-night doubleheader and second-year left-hander Greg Mathews worked six innings of another shutout, 3-0, in the nightcap.

OCT. 9 1987 FORSCH NAILS LEONARD

SAN FRANCISCO

THE CARDINALS, WITH 202 RUNS BATTED IN SITTING ON THE BENCH, were looking at a 4-0 deficit after five innings. Their chances of winning the third game of the National League Championship Series looked about as good as Mr. Ed's at Pimlico.

But Jim Lindeman's two-run homer off Atlee Hammaker in the sixth got the Cardinals back into the game. They scored four runs off Hammaker and Don Robinson in the seventh, featuring a two-run single by Vince Coleman past a drawn-in infield, and pulled out a 6-5 victory for a 2-1 edge in the best-of-seven series.

The winning pitcher was Bob Forsch, perhaps in more ways than one.

Without Jack Clark (106 RBIs) and Terry Pendleton (96 RBIs), who were nursing injuries to opposite ankles, the Cardinals were a lackluster loser through five innings. But in the bottom of the fifth, Forsch hit Jeffrey Leonard in the right shoulder with a pitch.

Forsch would never say that he was trying to drill Leonard, and manager Whitey Hezog said, "It was almost a strike. It was a hit-and-run and (Leonard) just went into the ball."

But the preliminary to this was Leonard's third homer in three games and his subsequent "one flap down" home run trot he displayed in the third inning as the Giants took their 4-0 lead.

The Cardinals had seemed annoyed by Leonard's antics when he employed his trot in St. Louis.

Ozzie Smith, who got three hits and made two outstanding defensive plays, said, "I don't know what you're talking about" when it was suggested that Forsch had awakened the Cardinals. But as he said that, Smith raised an eyebrow.

"It's a good thing I wasn't pitching," Smith said.

Tom Herr said, "In that situation, you don't want to hit a guy. But if you are, it's

The Giants' Jeffrey Leonard warms up for a playoff series in which he causes a flap with his "one flap down" home run trot.

nice that it was him."

As for Leonard, he said long after the game, "Somebody will pay."

Herzog pointed more to what happened later in the fifth inning, when Forsch pitched out of a bases-loaded, one-out situation by getting Chili Davis to pop up and Will Clark to fly out.

"He saved the game for us," Herzog said. "If they score any more, we're out of it."

In the next inning, Lindeman, batting fourth for only the second time this season, ripped a two-run homer and the Cardinals had seized momentum.

"This is the greatest thing that has happened to me in the major leagues," Lindeman said.

Joe Magrane was tagged for three runs in the second inning, and the Candlestick Park fans were treated to another "arm flap" homer by Leonard in the third.

Leonard, tying a playoff record by homering in three successive games, drilled a Magrane pitch over the left-field fence and trotted ever so slowly around the bases with his arm rigid at his left side. Leonard, an admirer of home-run trots executed by Pedro Guerrero and Dave Parker, calls the flap "part of my creativity."

The game's first part of high drama occurred in the fifth when Herzog sent ex-Giant Jack Clark to pinch-hit with Tony Pena and Tom Lawless on base and two out.

Clark took a strike, then missed on a vicious swing. The Candlestick Park crowd rose to its feet and created an almost unbelievable din for a fifth-inning situation.

After throwing a ball, Hammaker stepped off the mound, and catcher Bob Brenly went out for a conference. At 2-2, Hammaker again stepped off and another meeting ensued.

Finally, with the fans chanting, "Beat Jack Clark," the Cardinals slugger was called out on strikes by Dave Pallone.

"I guess they came prepared," said Clark. "Did 57,000 people meet in the parking lot or what?"

Action was heated in the bottom of the fifth, too, when with first base occupied, reliever Forsch drilled Leonard on a 1-1 pitch. Leonard glared at Forsch and might have yelled something as he ran to first base.

The Giants loaded the bases when Herr couldn't hold onto a flip by Smith after the Cardinals' shortstop had come in to field Candy Maldonado's roller. But Forsch pitched out of trouble.

The victory was the first for Forsch at Candlestick since Aug. 28, 1979. "This is the first game I've won here since some of these guys were in junior high school," he said.

Whitey Herzog walks away after losing an argument with umpire Dave Pallone.

▲ As catcher Tony Pena heads for the dugout, Lindeman congratulates reliever
Todd Worrell, who gets the save in the Cards' comeback win.

◀ Ozzie Smith waits to congratulate Jim Lindeman on his two-run homer, which
gets the Cardinals back into a game they eventually win.

▲ A Cardinals fan makes fun of Leonard's
uniform number.

COMMISH'S MOMENT

ALTHOUGH VETERAN BOB FORSCH LED THE TEAM in starts for the season, Whitey Herzog left him out of the four-man playoff rotation. But Forsch still made his mark — on the right shoulder of Jeffrey Leonard.

Leonard had irritated the Cardinals and their fans with his "one flap down" home-run trot in St. Louis. When he pulled the stunt again in San Francisco, trotting ever so slowly around the bases with his arm rigid at his left side following a homer off Joe Magrane, relief pitcher Forsch took matters into his own hands.

Of course, Forsch said the pitch that hit Leonard had "slipped." But his teammates got the message and rallied from four runs down for the key win in a seven-game series.

MAY 15 1988 — SECRET WEAPON ON THE HILL

IN ONE OF THE MOST IMPROBABLE BASEBALL GAMES ever played at Busch Stadium, consider this most improbable box-score entry: Losing pitcher — Oquendo.

Infielder and utilityman Jose Oquendo pitched three scoreless innings of relief as the eighth Cardinals pitcher, but Atlanta's Ken Griffey finally beat him and the Cardinals 7-5 with a two-run double in the 19th inning.

Griffey's double came with two outs after walks to Dion James and Dale Murphy and after Cardinals manager Whitey Herzog had repositioned right fielder Tom Brunansky and left fielder Jose DeLeon — yes, Jose DeLeon — for the 11th time.

DeLeon, a pitcher, went to left field in the 16th, when Oquendo moved from first base to the mound, because the Cardinals were out of reserves.

The Cardinals used 23 players, all except Sunday's starting pitcher, Larry McWilliams, in the 5-hour 40-minute game. DeLeon played outfield for four innings and pitcher John Tudor batted for him in the 19th.

Oquendo, who allowed six walks and four hits, could have been a winning pitcher in the 18th. The Cardinals had the bases loaded with one out, but Duane Walker's broken-bat liner doubled Brunansky off third base. The Cardinals left 21 men on base.

Oquendo's loss was the first decision for a non-registered pitcher in the major leagues since 1968, when that noted New York Yankees reliever, Rocco Colavito, beat the Detroit Tigers with 2 2/3 innings of relief.

Oquendo had pitched one inning last year in Philadelphia, giving up three runs.

"I was trying to get back for last year," Oquendo said. "They hit the ball pretty hard, but this is a big park. It could have been over anywhere else.

"I'm glad I got the chance to pitch. I'm glad nobody got hurt. It was fun for everyone, and that's all that matters. I'd like to have won, but there's

In a game against Atlanta that goes 19 innings, utilityman Jose Oquendo ends up as the losing pitcher.

Dubbed "The Secret Weapon," Jose Oquendo in 1988 becomes the first National Leaguer in 70 years to play all nine positions in one season.

nothing we can do."

Herzog sent Oquendo to the mound when Randy O'Neal hurt his arm in the 15th, his only inning. Herzog said Tom Lawless, who was in the game at third base, would have pitched the 20th inning.

Catcher Steve Lake said that when the two went over their signals before the start of the 16th inning, Oquendo said he had three pitches.

"I started chuckling," Lake said. "Then I see that he's dead serious."

"He threw a lot of sliders and a lot of split-fingers. I never knew where his fastball was going. I didn't know if he was going to drop down (sidearm) or throw overhand."

Home-plate umpire Bob Davidson, who must have called 700 pitches, said of the evening, "It got to be kind of comical.

"Whitey said he was bringing in Oquendo to pitch and he said, 'Can I forfeit?' I said, 'Whitey, you can do what you want to do.' "

Herzog moved Brunansky and DeLeon a total of 11 times in four innings, and DeLeon actually caught two fly balls, both in right field. Griffey served his game-winning double to left, where DeLeon had no chance.

The Braves' Dale Murphy said of Oquendo, "The guy had good stuff. He threw me some great forkballs. But if he had beaten us, I wouldn't have known what to say."

Winning pitcher Rick Mahler, who pitched eight scoreless innings, said, "Give the guy a lot of credit. He showed a lot of guts. But I said to myself, 'I'm not going to lose to this guy.' "

COMMISH'S MOMENT

ONE OF THE GREAT SIDELIGHTS of this game was that it went well after midnight Saturday – or after several of the downtown restaurants and watering holes had closed for the night.

There were no 3 a.m. closings in the city, and there was no "last call" yet on beer sales at the ballpark. So customers began streaming into Busch after midnight to watch "Secret Weapon" Oquendo pitch . . . or maybe it was to quaff a cold one or two.

The next afternoon, Whitey Herzog asked Oquendo if he could play center field since Willie McGee was ailing. Oquendo was too much of a team man to say no, even though he barely could raise his arm above his waist, and he threw virtually sidearm from center field.

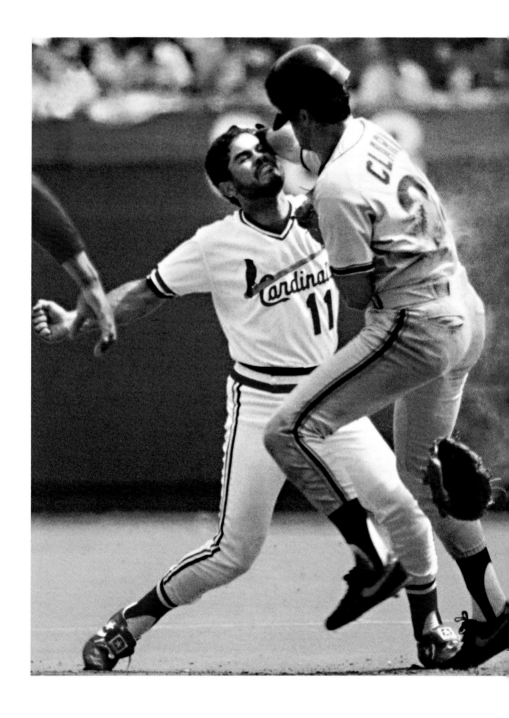

JULY 24 1988 BOUT WITH WILL CLARK

SAN FRANCISCO'S RICK REUSCHEL WAS ON HIS WAY to his 25th career shutout when suddenly, a hockey game broke out at Busch Stadium.

Reuschel eventually would get a 5-0 shutout over the Cardinals, but not before there were two bench-clearing incidents in the eighth inning, including one honest-to-goodness baseball fight.

The Cardinals had two lightweights in the ring — Jose Oquendo and Ozzie Smith — against San Francisco heavyweight Will Clark. Just when the Giants-Cardinals rivalry, spawned by a bench-clearer here two Julys ago, is kicking up again, the season series is over.

"I don't think we'll be seeing them in October," Cardinals manager Whitey Herzog said, referring to the teams' respective standings in the National League.

"A break for the umpires," crew member Dutch Rennert said.

The brawl started in the eighth inning when Candy Maldonado grounded to Smith with one out. Clark, running from first, made contact with second baseman Oquendo by sliding into him about six to eight feet past the bag after the forceout.

As Oquendo and Smith loomed over Clark, the following scenario took place:

Oquendo kicked Clark and then cuffed Clark's helmet with his hand. Clark, his attention having been obtained, jumped to his feet and grabbed Oquendo.

Smith, coming to the rescue, landed a punch from behind and then missed a roundhouse punch. Smith got in two more blows as Oquendo and Clark continued grappling, with Clark gaining the upper hand.

Maldonado, flying in from the right side, apparently gave Smith a shot that split Smith's lip. Tom Pagnozzi, who came from the Cardinals' bullpen, wrestled Maldonado to the ground.

Meantime, two more Cardinals, third baseman Terry Pendleton and

Cardinals second baseman Jose Oquendo ends up tangling with the Giants' Will Clark after taking exception to Clark's wide-ranging slide into second.

reliever Scott Terry, had joined the fray to try to serve as peacemakers and the Giants' Mike Aldrete had taken Smith to the ground.

Crew chief Frank Pulli finally got hold of Smith, who was having subsequent jawing sessions with the Giants' Bob Brenly, an old favorite of his, and Chris Speier.

Terry was to be involved again two pitches later. His first pitch to Aldrete was high and outside and the second pitch was high and very inside. Home-plate umpire Randy Marsh ejected Terry because he thought it was an obvious brushback pitch and the Giants bench emptied again. The Cardinals bench quickly followed suit.

This time, Brenly and Smith were engaged in verbal abuse near the third-base bag but there were no punches thrown. The rest of the game continued without incident, although there were police on the field.

Oquendo said, "I was just trying to get out of the way and I didn't think that was a right slide. (Clark) slid late. I was ticked off."

Clark had slid hard into second two nights before on a potential double-play ball and Herzog had questioned second-base umpire Marsh's call then.

"Both times, there's no dirt where he slid on the first-base side of the bag," Herzog said.

"The rule states that you can slide on the first-base side of the bag and your momentum can carry you on that side of the bag. But you cannot break up a double play and your first mark be on the other side of the bag. They didn't call it, so (Clark) did it again. I told them if they had called it the other night, this stuff wouldn't have happened."

Of Oquendo's and Smith's retaliations, Herzog said, "Any shortstop and second baseman would do the same thing. You can get your knees hurt bad."

When Herzog's complaint was repeated to Rennert, he said, "(Clark) didn't slide out of the baseline. He slid over the base. Straight and directly. A hard slide. Baseball can be a hard game. He's got a gripe, but . . . that's all you've got to do — slide directly over the bag."

Pagnozzi said Clark should have expected something to happen to him.

"Jose was doing what he's got to do," Pagnozzi said. "If Will Clark continues to slide like that, somebody will take care of him. It's just a matter of time. Nobody slides that far through the bag. He's going to get somebody hurt if he doesn't get hurt before. Somebody might drop down (on a throw) and smoke his noggin."

As for others who might have been occupied during the main event, pitcher Joe Magrane said he was talking to his stockbroker and Dan Quisenberry said he was playing Henry Kissinger. He said he confronted an opponent but declined battle "because he looked like Mike Tyson."

COMMISH'S MOMENT

DUTCH RENNERT, THE SECOND-BASE UMPIRE this day, was considered among the best ball-and-strike arbiters. But he missed something in the brawl.

Ozzie Smith, rushing to the defense of Jose Oquendo, threw a wild, roundhouse punch which missed its mark, and a few slaps that didn't. But he wasn't ejected, as Oquendo and Will Clark were, because Rennert said he didn't see it.

It took 12 years, but Oquendo and Clark eventually buried the hatchet. When Clark joined the Cardinals late in the 2000 season from Baltimore, he and Oquendo, who had become a Cardinals coach, reminisced about the 1988 scuffle.

JULY 6 1990 HERZOG GIVES UP

SAN DIEGO

WHITEY HERZOG QUIT A BASEBALL JOB for the first time in his life when he resigned as manager of the Cardinals with 2½ years remaining on his contract.

"I still enjoy managing," Herzog said. "But I just don't feel like I've done the job. I feel like I've underachieved. I can't get the guys to play."

Herzog, who will be a club vice president for the remainder of his contract, has been manager of the Cardinals since June 1980. That excludes the last five weeks of the 1980 season, when Red Schoendienst took over as Herzog became general manager. The next year, Herzog hired himself back as manager.

Schoendienst, 67, will take over as interim manager this time, too. The Cardinals, picked by some observers to win the National League Eastern Division, were 33-47 and in last place in the division when Herzog quit. They have been in last place for 56 days this season.

Herzog said that he was hoping to delay his decision as long as he could, but found that he was unable to get his team to play any better.

"That's the first time that I've ever felt like that in 17 years of managing," he said. "Even the bad years we had here, I felt I squeezed every ounce out of them.

"Even at Texas (in 1973), we were losing, but we were getting better."

Herzog, 58, said that about three weeks ago he suggested to general manager Dal Maxvill and Fred Kuhlmann, the club's chief executive officer, that he resign. Kuhlmann and Maxvill then talked Herzog out of it.

Herzog said he had been hopeful the club could "shake things up" by making a major trade. But the Cardinals were unable to make such a deal.

"I feel very bad for the ballclub, for the organization and for the fans," Herzog said. "I'm the manager. I take full responsibility."

But pitcher John Tudor said, "He shouldn't have to motivate this club. This club should motivate itself, and it hasn't. We haven't played very well.

 Whitey Herzog resigns as manager, saying, "I just felt I wasn't getting it done."

We've messed up every aspect of the game. We've messed it up every way possible. It's really a sorry sight to watch. I can't blame him at all for leaving."

Kuhlmann and Maxvill also attended the press conference to announce Herzog's resignation, and Maxvill said, "I don't want to dwell on the negatives of Whitey's leaving the Cardinals. I'm elated he's going to stay on in the organization. I'm happy to have him to rely on. He's been a prince to me, from the bottom of my heart."

Herzog said he informed his wife, Mary Lou, two days earlier of his decision, after the Cardinals had been swept in a three-game series in San Francisco. He left San Diego for St. Louis on the Anheuser-Busch plane, without stopping in the clubhouse.

Herzog took over a sixth-place club in 1980, succeeding Ken Boyer. The Cardinals won three National League titles — in 1982, 1985 and 1987 — in his tenure and one World Series, in 1982.

"I came here in last place, and I leave here in last place," Herzog said jokingly. "I left them right where I started."

Herzog will continue to get his base salary of $500,000 this year and a base salary of $550,000 for 1991 and 1992.

"I've really got the best of both worlds," said Herzog, who has an agreement with Kuhlmann that if a managing job to his liking comes up, he can take it at any time in the next two years.

"Fred honored my contract, which he didn't have to do. That was pretty darn nice of him. I can't say anything bad about anybody in the Cardinal organization."

But, Herzog added, "I don't want to manage this year, and I don't think I want to manage next year.

"It isn't that I can't stand losing if I think the club is playing up to its capabilities. I'm just bewildered. I can't believe this team is playing as bad as this team is playing. It's really been bad. I just felt I wasn't getting it done."

Herzog left with a career mark of 822-728 as Cardinals manager. Since the end of the 1987 season, after the team lost Jack Clark, the Cardinals were 195-209.

"We really got the short end of the stick," said Herzog, referring to free agency. "We lost (Bruce) Sutter. We lost Clark. Last year, we lost (Tony) Pena, but that was our doing because we thought (Todd) Zeile was ready. But we have lost three pretty good players."

Herzog thought the Cardinals' style of play, and that of other teams, had changed over the years.

"In 1982, we were more team-oriented. Most of our ballplayers were young — Ozzie Smith, Tommy Herr, Keith Hernandez was in about his fifth year.

"All of a sudden, team ball is gone. A guy might act like he's giving himself up, but it doesn't happen.

"But I don't think you can go to a player in his (free-agent) year and get on him for not hitting the ball to the right side when he might hit .290 instead of .300."

Maxvill said he would begin compiling a list of managerial candidates immediately.

But one of Herzog's parting shots was, "I think almost anybody in this room can manage this club better than I can."

COMMISH'S MOMENT

A COUPLE OF DAYS BEFORE WHITEY HERZOG QUIT, the Cardinals — who had many players in the "walk" years of their contracts — played a particularly desultory game at San Francisco, making three errors in a 9-2 loss to the Giants. Herzog was upset when he saw some of the players laughing on the bench during the game.

Afterward, having watched the same poor play he had, I said to Herzog, "Where do I go to resign?", not knowing that he was going to do precisely that two days later.

The announcement was made late on a Friday morning in San Diego. Herzog invited the scribe to his hotel suite and said, "Want a beer?" I declined, but he said, "Hell, I can have one. I'm not managing any more."

Mark Whiten holds the four balls he hit for home runs in a 12-RBI game against the Reds.

<table>
<tr><td>

SEPT. 7 1993
</td><td>

WHITEN'S 4-HOMER GAME
</td></tr>
</table>

CINCINNATI

IN AN ABYSMAL PERFORMANCE, the Cardinals and Cincinnati Reds set a major-league record for most pitchers used in a nine-inning game when they combined for 15 in a 14-13 Cincinnati victory in the opener of a twi-night doubleheader.

But that was nothing compared to what Cardinals outfielder Mark Whiten had in store in the nightcap.

Whiten did something no Cardinal had done — not Stan Musial, Joe Medwick or Johnny Mize — when he became the 12th player in history to hit four home runs in a game. He also became only the second player in history to drive in 12 runs in a game — tying Jim Bottomley of the 1924 Cardinals — as the Cards blasted the Reds 15-2.

A first-inning grand slam by Whiten, who hadn't homered since Aug. 11, helped propel Bob Tewksbury to his 16th win. That homer came off rookie Larry Luebbers. Whiten also popped three-run homers off rookie Mike Anderson in the sixth and seventh innings. In the ninth, he tagged Rob Dibble with his fourth homer, a 441-foot drive over the center-field wall.

"I was impressed with that one," Whiten said.

Sixteen of Whiten's 22 homers — and all four in this game — came while batting lefthanded, which manager Joe Torre said is Whiten's "weak side."

"This is the top of the list for me," Torre said. "This is the No. 1 achievement I've ever witnessed."

Whiten, 26, didn't allow himself to get too excited about the achievement until after the game. His teammates had spread a red carpet of equipment bags, and when Whiten came up the steps to the clubhouse, they formed a two-sided line and raised their bats in salute, chanting, "Hard Hittin' Mark Whiten.' "

Upon finally arriving at his locker, Whiten found a couple of bottles of champagne. He carried a bag with the four balls he hit over the wall. "None of them carried into the seats," he said. "The ground crew guys got them for me."

Ironically, Whiten had been at the focal point of the first game when Reggie Sanders' liner in the ninth hooked, then sank and got away from Whiten as the winning run scored.

"He was buried in his locker after that first game," Torre said. "Not that the ball got away from him but the fact that we lost. He takes losses as hard as anybody on this ballclub."

Just before Whiten's third home run, Bernard Gilkey had dashed home from second on an infield hit by Gerald Perry. Had Gilkey stayed at third, Whiten could have had 13 RBIs. But Whiten said, "How do you know I would have hit a home run if he had stayed at third?"

Gilkey said he knew Whiten was "definitely into the zone."

"I was talking to him in the outfield after he hit his third one and it was almost like he didn't see me. He looked straight through me."

Whiten agreed that he had found that certain "zone," although he said, "You don't really know you're in a zone until after the game. I think my teammates knew it before I did. But it didn't matter where the ball was."

On the last at-bat, Dibble ran the count to 2-0 and Whiten said, "I felt he was going to try to pitch around me."

But Dibble came after Whiten with a fastball, and Whiten drilled it. All the home runs came on fastballs, which makes one wonder why teams don't throw Whiten more breaking balls.

"I wasn't going to walk him. I've walked enough people lately," Dibble said. "I'm happy for Mark Whiten. He's a part of history. And so am I."

Fans saluted Whiten on his last trip around the bases, bowing over the Cardinals' dugout. He was given a curtain call, although only about 2,000 fans remained at midnight.

After Whiten cracked the champagne, he was going back to the hotel to watch SportsCenter on ESPN. "Maybe it will put me to sleep, but I doubt it," he said.

"I don't have words to explain this. It's amazing. Every time I hit it, I was kind of amazed."

One more record that Whiten tied was RBIs for a doubleheader at 13. In an 0-for-four first game, Whiten drove in one run. The other 12 enabled him to tie St. Louisan Nate Colbert of the 1972 San Diego Padres.

COMMISH'S MOMENT

HAVING STRUGGLED THROUGH a 3 hour 41 minute marathon in the first game of the twi-nighter, I wasn't prepared for Whiten's heroics in the nightcap.

Until he came to bat in the sixth, he had homered only once. But he homered in the sixth, eighth and ninth — Rob Dibble laid in a meatball pitch for him in the ninth — and suddenly Whiten was in the history books. But he really didn't seem to grasp the moment.

A couple days later in San Francisco, manager Joe Torre brought Whiten into his office to meet Hall of Famer Willie Mays, who also had hit four homers in a game. Upon leaving Torre's office to return to the clubhouse, Whiten was asked how the meeting went. "He's just another man," said Whiten.

SEPT 2 1996 | GOLDEN OLDIES OZZIE & WILLIE

THEY ARE LONG IN THE TOOTH, but more important, long in pennant race experience. And if there were any doubt there's a pennant race, it should have been erased by the frenetic goings-on at Busch Stadium on Labor Day afternoon.

Ozzie Smith, 41, tied his career high by scoring four runs, one of them on a rare home run. Willie McGee, 37, had four hits and three runs batted in, the last hit scoring Smith from second base as the Cardinals rallied to beat the Houston Astros 8-7 in 10 grinding innings over 4 hours and 1 minute.

The Cardinals, who have won four in a row after losing three in a row, moved to one-half game behind the Astros in the National League Central.

Smith slid home safely just ahead of center fielder Brian Hunter's strong throw after Hunter had fielded McGee's chopper up the middle. Moments before, Smith thought he had won the game with a single to left. But 21-year-old pinch runner Miguel Mejia took a wide turn at third and was cut down at the plate. Smith alertly went to second on the play.

"It was only the second out," Houston manager Terry Collins said. "I didn't think that we were off the hook until after the third out."

Collins was right. For the second day in succession, the Cardinals came from four runs behind to win a game, prompting owners Drew Baur, Fred Hanser and David Pratt to burst into manager Tony La Russa's office to offer congratulations.

Presidential candidate Bob Dole and running mate Jack Kemp didn't know what they were missing by leaving the game early.

"When we were losing early," outfielder Brian Jordan said, "Ozzie and Willie kept telling us to keep fighting and keep competing. They said it would boil down to the last inning. When I saw Ozzie get to second base,

 In what turns out to be his last season, Ozzie Smith, 41, shows flashes of the brilliance that once was routine by hitting .282 in 1996 and helping the Cardinals win their first division title in nine years.

I had a feeling someone was going to be a hero."

In five games between the clubs that have been played in the past 10 days, the Cardinals are 3-2. They've scored 14 runs and given up 16. "It was an outstanding competition," said La Russa.

"We've played this club five times with first place at stake. There hasn't been a bad game yet."

Smith hasn't had many bad games lately either. Playing more and more as the season — and his career — wind down, Smith is hitting .294. He, like fellow golden oldie McGee, drove in three runs.

"I'm going out, hopefully, the way I came in," said Smith. "I've always tried to respect this game. I've given my all each and every day.

"Given the opportunity, I could probably still play another two or three years — given the opportunity. All I can ask for is the opportunity. Willie and I are doing what we know we can do and have been asked to do."

This is the first pennant race for Smith in seven years. "I think everybody should be juiced up in a pennant race," he said. "If you don't, then you shouldn't be here."

The Astros threatened in the 10th with the game tied 7-7, but La Russa earned some of his salary. With a runner at second and two out, La Russa brought in righthanded rookie Alan Benes for his first professional relief appearance.

Collins countered with pinch-hitter Tony Eusebio, a .443 career hitter against the Cardinals. La Russa intentionally walked Eusebio, even though it meant facing lefthanded-hitting Derrick May as a pinch hitter. But La Russa knew that May had been bothered by an abdominal strain and might not be able to catch up to Benes' fastball. He didn't, striking out to end the inning.

By walking Eusebio, La Russa also got hard-throwing closer John Hudek out of the game after just one inning, with twilight looming.

Smith paid La Russa this compliment: "That was a beautiful thing. That might have been the turning point."

Darryl Kile, who has a 6.43 earned-run average against the Cardinals, was torched for 11 hits and five runs in five innings. But Kile still had the four-run lead until Smith lined his second homer of the season — both lefthanded — after Terry Bradshaw's two-out pinch single in the fourth.

"Willie and I are just doing what we do," Smith said. "That's what we get paid for, what we've been doing for years."

 It's hats off to Willie McGee, who at age 37 reaches the 2,000-hit plateau in 1996.

▲ Smith, Whitey Herzog and Bruce Sutter enjoy reminiscing about some of the "good old days" – the 1982 World Series.

◀ Even in the twilight of their careers, Ozzie Smith (left) and Willie McGee put smiles on the faces of Cardinals fans.

COMMISH'S MOMENT

THE SIX RBIS BY OZZIE SMITH AND WILLIE MCGEE, both no longer regular players, represented both a blast from the past and a recurring theme through 1996.

The challenging Astros just couldn't beat the Cardinals in Tony La Russa's first season, losing all six meetings at Busch Stadium and 11 of 13 for the year.

Ozzie would play only two more months, retiring after the Cardinals' ugly exit in the National League Championship Series against Atlanta. But McGee also played until he was 40, ending his second tour with the Cardinals in 1999.

Mark McGwire wipes away a tear at a press conference where he announces plans to start the Mark McGwire Charitable Foundation for sexually and physically abused children.

SEPT. 16 1997	# BIG MAC'S BIG NIGHT

FOR ANYONE WONDERING WHAT ALL THE EXCITEMENT was about with the Cardinals signing Mark McGwire to a new contract, it took one swing to show it.

In his first at-bat of a game that followed his afternoon press conference, McGwire slammed a home run above the scoreboard in left field at Busch Stadium, the longest homer ever measured at the ballpark. He got a standing ovation before and after the 517-foot blast, as Cardinals fans showed their support for a deal wrapped up earlier in the day that left everyone involved happy.

"This was the most pleasant salary negotiation that any team has ever had with a player," said Drew Baur, one of the Cardinals owners.

McGwire, the slugging first baseman who has fallen in love with the St. Louis fans as much as they have with him since he was acquired from the Oakland Athletics on July 31, signed for three years and $28.5 million with an option for a fourth year at $11 million.

One provision of the contract is that McGwire, who now has 52 home runs — 18 in the 1 1/2 months since the Cardinals swapped him for three pitchers — will receive a $1 million signing bonus.

Another, at McGwire's request, is that he will donate $1 million each year to a new Mark McGwire Charitable Foundation for sexually and physically abused children.

The charity is so close to McGwire's heart that he broke down at the podium during the press conference as he discussed it. He said a couple of his close friends had been victims of abuse as youths.

McGwire's arrival — and his towering home runs — delighted crowds and ignited fan interest in a year when the Cardinals stumbled, trailing division-leading Houston by 10 games earlier in the summer.

Primary owner Bill DeWitt Jr., who made the announcement of the contract agreement, said: "Mark is reminiscent of the great Cardinals of the past. Players like Johnny Mize, Red Schoendienst, Stan Musial, Enos Slaughter, Bob Gibson, Lou Brock, Ozzie Smith. These were not only impact players but also great team players with a burning desire to win."

However, the 6-foot-5 McGwire is unlike any home-run hitter the Cardinals ever had. Last week, he joined Babe Ruth as one of only two players in major-league history to hit 50 or more homers in back-to-back seasons.

Both sides indicated that McGwire, 33, might have received more had he filed for free agency after the season, as he had intended since he came from Oakland.

"There's a lot of money being passed around . . . of people looking for the last dollar. I can assure you that Mark McGwire did not do that," general manager Walt Jocketty said. "He accepted less money to play in St. Louis than he probably would have got on the free agent market. I think that's an indication of the type of person we have here.

"I thought all along that if we got Mark here, we could show him what it was like to be a Cardinal and the tradition of this organization. And I think we've won him over."

McGwire has agreed to defer about 25 percent of his salary every year to be paid after his retirement so that the Cardinals can either retain some of their own talent or seek new players to be competitive.

"I'll do anything I can to enable them to get the players they want to get by structuring my contract a certain way," McGwire said.

Using a word he often has employed since he arrived, McGwire said, "I'm definitely overwhelmed with the contract. I don't think it was too hard to fall in love with St. Louis. This is what everybody was talking about when I came over. I'll tell you what: It makes me float every time I come to the ballpark and play in front of these fans. I've never been treated that way as a baseball player. This is just unbelievable.

"I'm proud to be a Cardinal. Yeah, when I first got here, sure I thought that I definitely would try the free-agent market. But as time wore on and I saw the talent of this team, that's what I looked at the most. Everybody

McGwire waves to fans after homering off the Dodgers' Ramon Martinez in his first at-bat after signing a three-year contract.

is in this game to win and we're definitely going to win here. I can't think of another place to play in major-league baseball."

The original thought was that McGwire would sign with a Southern California team to be closer to his son Matt, who will turn 10 next week and who lives with his mother.

But the youngest McGwire visited here last month and liked the city. When McGwire called him and told him about the contract, Matt McGwire said, "All right."

COMMISH'S MOMENT

WHEN MCGWIRE BROKE DOWN AT HIS PRESS CONFERENCE as he talked about child abuse, we all wondered if he had been abused. But he indicated that it had happened to somebody he knew well.

McGwire's home run in the first inning that night was the forerunner of his ability to homer almost on demand over the next two-plus seasons. But each home run fueled the media's fire, and McGwire became a much bigger target in St. Louis than he ever had imagined. After all, nobody really had hit many home runs as a Cardinal in a long time.

Following his first burst of homers, McGwire said with some exasperation, "When I came here from Oakland, they told me the only guy I had to talk to was you." I responded, "Well, then, don't hit so many home runs!"

▲ Mark McGwire watches home run No. 62 leave the ballpark.

SEPT. 8 1998 | JUBILATION: MCGWIRE'S NO. 62

THE PRODUCTION WAS THE SUMMER OF 62. The star was Mark McGwire. The reviews were off the charts at Busch Stadium.

McGwire's shortest homer of the season, 341 feet, engendered the loudest, longest roar of this or many other seasons. McGwire's fourth-inning, first-pitch liner over the left-field wall off Chicago Cubs righthander Steve Trachsel was his 62nd homer, breaking the most hallowed record in baseball. The record had been held since 1961 by the late Roger Maris, who finished his career with the Cardinals but had 61 homers with the New York Yankees in '61.

Ironically, before the 6-3 Cardinals victory, both McGwire and home-run rival Sammy Sosa of the Cubs got to swing the 61st home-run bat belonging to Maris, which had been taken out of the Hall of Fame and brought here.

McGwire rubbed the bat on his chest and, according to Donald Marr, president of the Hall of Fame, said, "I hope you're with me tonight."

McGwire brought both bats with him to the postgame interview session.

With tears welling in his eyes, McGwire said, "I touched it. I touched it with my heart. Now I can honestly say my bat's going right next to his and I'm damned proud of it."

After he hit his seventh homer in seven games, McGwire almost missed first base before coach Dave McKay, into whose arms McGwire had jumped, helped rescue him.

"When I hit the ball, I thought it was a line drive and I thought it was going to hit the wall and the next thing I knew, it disappeared," said McGwire. "I had to go back and touch it. I can honestly say that's the first time I ever had to go back and do that."

Then he accepted congratulations of all four Cubs infielders. As he came down the third-base line, McGwire tapped his heart and pointed to the sky to show Maris that Maris was indeed with him.

Before he touched home, McGwire shook hands with and embraced

 McGwire's home run feat sends Cardinal Nation into a cheering frenzy.

Cubs catcher Scott Servais. In the various celebrations, which took 11 minutes, McGwire lifted and hugged his son Matthew three times. He also hugged several other Cardinals and even Sosa, who came in from right field to edge into the pileup near the plate.

McGwire gave Sosa the traditional Cardinal home-run ritual of two fists popping and then punches to the abdomen. Then they exchanged the Sosa ritual of two fingers going to the lips and heart in honor of his mother and former broadcaster Harry Caray.

"It was a sweet, sweet run around the bases," said McGwire.

"I was trying to imagine what it was going to feel like doing that. I sure the heck was floating.

"I hope I didn't act foolish, but this was history."

At one point, McGwire was handed a microphone and he thanked the St. Louis fans. Another ironic note: McGwire officially could begin thanking the St. Louis fans because attendance kicked past 2.8 million for the season. Any paid admission over 2.8 million nets McGwire a dollar a head.

He also hopped into the box seats to embrace the Maris children. "Like I said, I touched Roger's bat and put it against my heart and that's the first

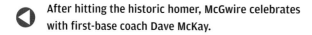 After hitting the historic homer, McGwire celebrates with first-base coach Dave McKay.

thing that came to my mind when I ran over there and told all four of them and it was just unbelievable," McGwire said.

The ball went into a storage area which used to be the visitors bullpen and it was recovered by a groundskeeper, Tim Forneris, who returned the ball to McGwire.

McGwire was honored with a postgame ceremony in which he received a red convertible from the Cardinals owners and a trophy from the commissioner's office, called the Commissioner's Historic Achievement Award.

Commissioner Bud Selig called the night "one of the most historic nights in baseball history. (St. Louis) is the crown jewel of baseball franchises."

Now that he owns baseball's most prestigious record, if not in all sports, McGwire said, "Absolutely incredible. I'm almost speechless.

"I've been talking about this since January," said McGwire, who agreed a significant weight had been removed from his shoulders. "I don't know how heavy the Arch is but the Arch is off my back now."

McGwire's homer was his 50th against righthanded pitching, and his

 McGwire seems to be watching in disbelief as he checks out a video board replay of No. 62.

32nd this year at Busch Stadium. He reached the 62-homer plateau in his 145th game. "Was it that quick?" asked McGwire.

"I'll tell you what, the last week-and-a-half, my stomach has been turning and my heart has been beating a million miles a minute. To do it that fast, I just don't know."

In 188 games as a Cardinal over two seasons, McGwire has hit an almost unimaginable 86 home runs. Because of what he has done and who he is, McGwire may be the player most responsible for bringing back the fans after the 1994 strike threatened to ruin the game.

McGwire said, "The whole country has been involved in this, I think since after the All-Star break. If people say it's bringing the country together, I'm happy to bring the country together."

But McGwire also said, "I hope my son one day grows up and becomes a baseball player and breaks it."

Fireworks erupt above Busch Stadium after McGwire's history-making homer.

With his arm on the shoulder of Roger Maris Jr., McGwire celebrates with jubilant fans.

COMMISH'S MOMENT

WITH THE CARDINALS leaving town after this game, Mark McGwire again accommodated the Busch Stadium faithful. And the great thing about the record-breaking homer was that we weren't even sure if McGwire was going to have the record three weeks later, what with Sammy Sosa making his charge.

Of course, McGwire may well have finished with 71 homers for the season. Second-base umpire Bob Davidson deprived him of one in Milwaukee in late September when he determined that a fan had reached over the wall to make contact with the ball.

Ray Lankford congratulates Albert Pujols after the rookie homers in his Busch Stadium debut.

APRIL 9 2001 | PUJOLS' HOME DEBUT

THE CARDINALS HOME OPENER with the Colorado Rockies was played at sea level and not in the mountains. One run at Coors Field is a bad inning. On an August-in-April day at Busch Stadium, one run was priceless.

Entering the ninth inning, the teams had traded two-run homers by Colorado's Larry Walker, who hit his while breaking his bat, and Cardinals rookie Albert Pujols, who is hitting his with a magic wand.

Then came a few of those "little things" that decide games, and when this one was over, the Cardinals had extended their winning streak to four with a 3-2 win in front of a sellout house of 48,702. Colorado has lost four straight since trouncing the Cardinals by a score of 32-11 in three games in Denver last week.

The winning run scored with one out in the ninth when Ray Lankford slid home as Rockies reliever Jose Jimenez, noted for his sinkerball, threw a four-seam fastball high and off the glove of catcher Brent Mayne while the Cardinals had the bases loaded.

Pujols put the Cardinals ahead in the second, driving a 1-2 Denny Neagle delivery into the left-field seats. Pujols has knocked in 10 runs in his past four games after starting the season one for nine.

The rookie received his first curtain call.

"These fans are very knowledgable," teammate Jim Edmonds said. "They know he's 21 years old and a rookie and to get a big hit in a game like that is a big deal."

La Russa watches how his veterans treat Pujols, and he said, "These guys love Albert Pujols. He's like the team pet. They would hurt somebody badly if they messed with him on the streets."

Pujols, who was a last-minute addition to the club in spring training, is "day to day," joked La Russa. "If he has one bad day, he's out of here — and I'm right behind him."

Colorado had threatened to break the tie in its ninth. Third-base coach Rich Donnelly, one of the most aggressive in the league, tried to score Jeff

Cirillo, an average runner, from first on a double by Ron Gant.

Edmonds, who is not moving at top speed with a bruised left toe and a sometimes balky right knee, got to the ball and fired toward cutoff man Edgar Renteria, the shortstop. The ball sailed past Renteria, but second baseman Fernando Vina was lined up correctly, moved his feet quickly and cut down Cirillo at home, where he tried to go around catcher Mike Matheny.

La Russa called the play "highlight material — just like we practiced in spring training. Nobody throws better than Jim Edmonds. Nobody — for strength and accuracy. And we have two middle infielders who are strong and accurate."

In the bottom of the ninth, Bobby Bonilla doubled off Gabe White. La Russa inserted J.D. Drew to run for Bonilla and had Ray Lankford bunt. Lankford had no sacrifices last year, and La Russa said, "I bet you he doesn't have five in his career.

"My highlight from all the stuff that happened today was Ray's bunt."

White's first pitch nearly sawed Lankford in half as he bunted it foul. He tried, half-heartedly, to convince home-plate umpire Robert Drake that he had been hit by the pitch, but Drake had none of it.

"It didn't touch me," Lankford said. "I was acting. I guess I didn't do a good job of acting."

Lankford got the next pitch down, and White threw to third, too late to catch Drew. Pujols was walked intentionally before Rockies second baseman Terry Shumpert made a magnificent diving stop on pinch-hitter Larry Sutton and, while sitting down, threw home to get Drew.

"When something like that happens, you think you're going to get out of it," Colorado manager Buddy Bell said.

But, with pinch-hitter Eli Marrero at bat, former Cardinal Jimenez's pitch eluded Mayne, and Lankford scored.

Because the Cardinals won, Pujols said: "Today, I feel more happy than after hitting my first home run in the big leagues. It's because of these fans and the way they treat you here — the way they love baseball."

Mark McGwire jokes with Pujols, who eventually replaces him as the Cardinals' first baseman.

 Pujols gets his first curtain call at Busch Stadium.

In his first game at Busch Stadium, Pujols bats
seventh and plays third base.

▲ Pujols caps his first major-league season by being
named the National League Rookie of the Year.

COMMISH'S MOMENT

On the same day that Albert Pujols hit his first Busch Stadium homer, he also drew the first intentional walk of his career in the ninth inning. Pujols batted in a lineup spot on this day where you probably never will see him again. He batted seventh and started the game at third base, but finished in right field.

You wonder how long it would have taken the Cardinals to bring up Pujols if Bobby Bonilla hadn't been hurt in the spring. Actually, it's amazing that Tony La Russa had even sent Pujols to the minors – briefly – after Mark McGwire had loomed behind La Russa during one exhibition game and threatened bodily harm to his manager if Pujols wasn't on the team.

 Matt Morris gets testy after being told that the Cubs may have tipped off
Sammy Sosa about the location of a pitch the slugger belts for a home run.

| MAY 8 2002 | **MATT'S SPAT WITH CUBS** |

CHICAGO

IT WASN'T, AS MANAGER TONY LA RUSSA POINTED OUT, that the Cardinals had been playing badly every inning of every game. One poor inning of every game had been enough to derail them.

But this time they pulled off the rare (for this season) feat of not having any bad innings. There was 10-strikeout starting pitching from Matt Morris, who didn't allow a hit from the third through the eighth innings against the Chicago Cubs. There was no-hit, one-inning relief from Jason Isringhausen. There was a brilliant backhand catch by left fielder Albert Pujols to bail Morris out of a two-on, two-out spot in the eighth.

And while the Cardinals, the leaders in men left on base in the major leagues, stranded 10 more runners, they were much more efficient offensively. They parlayed two sacrifice flies, a sacrifice bunt and a stolen base to set up all their runs in their 3-2 victory.

"We did today what we hadn't been doing," said La Russa, whose team is 15-19. "We played a really sound baseball game in every department. When you don't beat yourself, you give yourself a chance to win."

Morris, tossing a season-high 126 pitches, gave up only Sammy Sosa's two-run homer in the first inning and a second-inning single by losing pitcher Juan Cruz. Morris' only mistake was the inside fastball that Sosa golfed into the mitt of a fan standing on Waveland Avenue behind the left-field wall.

But pitching coach Dave Duncan suggested that Sosa might have had a little help from one of the Cubs' base coaches, either first-base coach Sandy Alomar or third-base coach Gene Glynn.

"Somebody on their team let him know locations," said Duncan. "We let them know we knew what they were doing and that it would be in their best interests to stop doing it." Or?

"They know what the 'or' is," said Duncan.

Cubs manager Don Baylor spoke in calm terms but was upset with Duncan's charge. "He's a liar," said Baylor.

"Sammy has hit 400-and-something (464) damn home runs. I could see

▲ Cardinals pitching coach Dave Duncan is not among Don Baylor's favorite rivals.

it if I'm stealing signs for (Augie) Ojeda." The young Cubs backup infielder has one career homer.

"We don't do that," Baylor continued. "Because, if you give location and if it's the wrong location, you want to get Sammy Sosa hit in the face looking for a breaking ball and (the pitcher) throws a fastball? You think one of those (coaches) at each corner wants to be wrong?

"I don't know why they think that. It's bull. It's paranoia, that's what it is. He's hit 60 homers three different times and he's got a lot bigger names than (Matt) Morris."

Morris responded, "It's bush-league baseball. The guy's an All-Star and they're tipping off location. Come on."

Then, in the heat of the moment, Morris said something he probably didn't mean. "Somebody might get a fastball in the ear if that's the way they want to do it," he said. "Someone's going to stick their nose over the plate and might take one in the ear. Come on. Play the game right."

To this, Baylor said, "Threats don't bother me.

"I've already warned my team about that kind of stuff. I said, 'Don't even fall for that.' We play this team way too many times and to get somebody hurt for bull, don't do it.

"I've seen (Duncan) do this too many different times with different people."

The teams resume hostilities, if that is the word, in five days in St. Louis. Scheduled starter for the Cardinals: Matt Morris.

▲ Mincing no words, Baylor answers Duncan's pitch-tipping charge by saying, "He's a liar."

COMMISH'S MOMENT

AFTER THE CARDINALS ACCUSED THE CUBS of tipping pitches, Matt Morris suggested he might have something extra for Sammy Sosa the next time around.

But when he faced the Cubs again five days later in St. Louis, Morris kept his composure. He gave up a single and a stolen base to Sosa in the first inning, but then gathered himself to throw a four-hit shutout.

Don Baylor was the manager of the Cubs at this time, but mistrust, even contempt, between the Cardinals and Cubs would actually escalate when Dusty Baker took over as manager in 2003.

JUNE 23 2002 PLAYING FOR DK

CHICAGO

A COMMON SIGHT IN THE CARDINALS' DUGOUT during games in which rookie Jason Simontacchi pitched was veteran Darryl Kile counseling Simontacchi after an inning or after he had been taken out of the game.

Only Kile's uniform was in the dugout as Simontacchi lost for the first time as a major leaguer in an 8-3 drubbing by Kerry Wood and the Chicago Cubs, the day after Kile died in his sleep at a Chicago hotel.

"It wasn't like he was constantly talking to me, but ... you want to go out there and do the best you can, knowing that's what Darryl would want," Simontacchi said. "Be it good, great, no-hitter or get beat up."

Simontacchi admitted the emotions had gotten to him.

"I told (pitching coach Dave) Duncan while I was walking out to the bullpen, 'I'm more nervous than I was before my first start,'" Simontacchi said. "It's been a rough 24 hours. And that's an understatement. It wasn't like DK was completely forgotten. You'd come in and you'd see his jersey hanging up. But it wasn't the regular dugout — the Cardinal dugout."

The Cardinals had talked about playing the game for Kile, who had been slated to start, but some of their spirit was gone when they hit the field.

Before the game, Cardinals center fielder Jim Edmonds said, "The best thing we could come up with as a team was to play the game for Darryl, play the game for us, play the game for the fans, play the game for baseball."

But after the game, he said that when he got to the field, "It was tougher than I thought. Much tougher. I felt (playing) was the right thing to do — until we got out there."

Catcher Mike Matheny, a close friend of Kile's, admitted he didn't really want to play in the game. "It shouldn't have been played," he said.

Manager Tony La Russa understood the sentiment.

◀ **Manager Tony La Russa says the decision to play as scheduled the day after pitcher Darryl Kile's death is "real life, ultra-difficult."**

"There's been a real tight bond," said La Russa, who had Mike DiFelice catch Simontacchi for the first time. "Maybe one or two guys down deep kind of disagreed with playing, but 20-plus and the manager and the coaches ... it was virtually unanimous.

"This is not phony dramatics. This is real life, ultra-difficult."

Cardinals left fielder Kerry Robinson had reservations about playing, even though he made a rare start. "I really didn't think we should have been out there," he said.

But Flynn Kile, Darryl's wife, had told the Cardinals during a religious service that morning that the Cardinals should go out and play. "She said one of the things she wanted us to do was win a World Series ring for DK," Robinson said.

Wrigley Field was full but there was a modicum of noise. There was no music between innings and a subdued version of "Take Me Out to the Ball Game" for the seventh-inning stretch.

"It was the same Wrigley crowd. But it was kind of odd not having any music," Robinson said.

Reliever Mike Timlin said, "It was very solemn. You hear some music and you get used to it. And the fans weren't even ragging on us. Even they kind of felt the sense that there was a piece missing."

But Timlin, who appeared in relief, said he thought the Cardinals gave their best effort.

"Knowing that today was DK's day (to start), you wanted to go out and pitch as he would pitch," Timlin said. "We wish we could have pulled it out, not just for us, but for him."

La Russa said Kile's absence was painfully obvious. "He started every fifth day but the other four days he was one of the guys in charge of the atmosphere we have," La Russa said. "You knew exactly where he'd be sitting on the bench at Wrigley, and yeah, you miss him. And it's going to happen over and over again."

At the end of the game, Cubs catcher Joe Girardi and some of his teammates shook hands with the Cardinals, something almost never done in baseball.

"It was a very sportsmanlike thing to do; really cool," Robinson said. "It showed a lot of class."

Girardi, who had to deliver the news the day before to a sold-out Wrigley crowd that the game had been postponed because of the Kile

Players and fans observe a moment of silence for Kile at Wrigley Field the day after the pitcher's unexpected death.

🔺 Catcher Mike Matheny touches his former batterymate's jersey as he heads to the locker room after sitting out a game he says "shouldn't have been played."

tragedy, said, "Everyone's going to grieve through this, but they have to try to carry on. In a sense, you play for Darryl. I believe that's probably what he'd want them to do. He'd want them to go out and win. You carry a responsibility if you're a St. Louis Cardinal."

The weight may be lifted someday but it'll take time.

"These last three days have seemed like a month," second baseman Fernando Viña said. "These last two days have seemed like one long day. You keep waiting for it to end."

Reflecting on the death of Kile (above), La Russa says: "You miss him. And it's going to happen over and over again."

▲ Zach Cole and Josh Blight, both of Florissant, Mo., join in the observance of 57 seconds of silence (Kile's uniform number was 57) before a game at Busch Stadium.

COMMISH'S MOMENT

YOU NEVER HAVE HEARD WRIGLEY FIELD SO QUIET. Fans from both sides still were reeling over the news of Kile's death the day before.

Catcher Mike Matheny, a close friend of Kile's, couldn't bring himself to play and Tony La Russa didn't try to force him. Jason Simontacchi, making the start Kile would have made, said he barely could handle the moment.

The Cardinals decided to play because Flynn Kile asked them to, but their effort was an excusably half-hearted one. Everyone was happy to leave Chicago.

Houston's Roger Clemens loses Game 7 of the 2004 NLCS to former teammate Jeff Suppan.

OCT. 21 2004 ROCKET GROUNDED

IN THE 100-YEAR HISTORY OF BASEBALL'S POSTSEASON PLAY, there have been only four seven-game series in which the home team has won every game. One came in 2001, when the Arizona Diamondbacks beat the New York Yankees.

The starting pitcher for the Yankees in Game 7 in 2001 was Roger Clemens, the same man who started in Game 7 of the Cardinals' National League Championship Series against the Houston Astros.

Clemens took a 2-1 lead into the sixth inning but was tagged for three runs as the Cardinals went ahead for good. The 5-2 victory made this not only the fourth seven-game series in which the home team won every game, but the first in the 19 years the LCS has been seven games.

The biggest headlines will go to Albert Pujols, who tied the game with a two-strike double to left, and Scott Rolen, who lined Clemens' next pitch just fair to left for a two-run homer.

But Clemens had as much or more trouble in the sixth with Cardinals reserve outfielder Roger Cedeño, who hadn't done so much as get the ball to the dirt part of the infield in five at-bats in this series.

Cedeño has a history with Clemens. In 25 career at-bats, Cedeño has 11 hits for a .440 average. The 11th hit was a leadoff single as a pinch hitter in the sixth, a ball that got past the dive of range-challenged second baseman Jeff Kent.

With Edgar Renteria at bat, Clemens tried to split his concentration by throwing a half-dozen times to first to keep Cedeño close while Renteria alternately went into sacrifice or hit-and-run mode.

Finally, Renteria bunted Cedeño to second and Larry Walker tapped out before Pujols and Rolen struck. But Cedeño already had done his part.

"He's the best," said Cedeño. "Every time you've got to concentrate because he's not going to give you a pitch to hit."

As for his having bothered Clemens while he was on base, Cedeño said, "He's been in this league for a long time. I might have bothered him a little bit. I wanted him to worry about me instead of worrying about the hitter."

After a visit from pitching coach Dave Duncan in the fourth inning, Suppan retires the next nine hitters.

Center fielder Jim Edmonds gives Suppan a helping hand with a spectacular diving catch to keep two Houston runs from scoring in the second inning.

Suppan lays down a squeeze bunt to drive in a run in the fourth inning.

First-base coach Dave McKay said Cedeño's lead was "one of those leads where it looks like he's going to go — and we may go. The lead gets the pitcher's attention and makes him focus on (the runner) and makes him rush to the plate.

"I think Clemens is too much of a veteran to let that bother him, but sometimes you're forced to rush and instead of that fastball being down and away, it might be over the plate."

Cardinals starter Jeff Suppan, a former teammate of Clemens in Boston, opposed his former tutor for the fifth time this season. Clemens was the winning pitcher in three of the first four, all won by the Astros.

Suppan's game was the same as it had been in his two previous playoff starts: Struggle early and then slam the door after hearing from pitching coach Dave Duncan.

Suppan served up a leadoff home run to slumping Craig Biggio on the fourth pitch of the game. In the second, center fielder Jim Edmonds saved Suppan with a miraculous diving catch off Brad Ausmus, snatching two runs from the Astros.

After Suppan hit Jeff Kent and allowed a single to Morgan Ensberg with nobody out in the fourth, he was visited by Duncan. In his two previous starts, when Suppan was staggering in the third inning, Duncan came to the mound and Suppan didn't allow a hit the rest of his time in the game.

Suppan again responded to the message, retiring the next nine hitters he faced, giving him 11 1/3 hitless innings after mound trips by Duncan.

Duncan said the message this time was "in order for his off-speed stuff to be effective, he had to get the ball in on the hitter for strikes."

Suppan achieved that — and now he finally has a victory over Clemens.

"I'm just happy to celebrate with these guys," Suppan said. "It's been a team effort all year long. We all pulled the rope. We had a goal in spring training, we talked about it and we really went about it as professionals and as a team."

Scott Rolen celebrates after hitting a two-run homer that proves to be the Game 7 winner.

 Relief pitcher Steve Kline and catcher Yadier Molina show their exhilaration over the team's Game 7 victory.

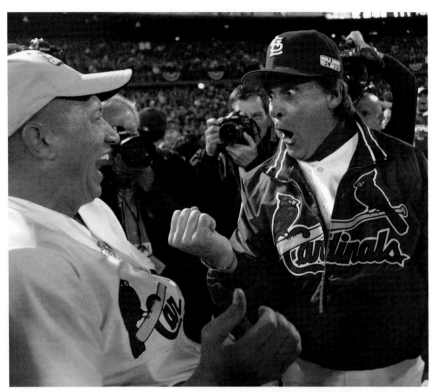

▲ Manager Tony La Russa reminds reliever Julian Tavarez he wasn't clowning around when he opted to let him face Houston slugger Carlos Beltran in the eighth inning.

COMMISH'S MOMENT

ONE RIGHT MOVE BY TONY LA RUSSA, and one risky move that turned out right, helped the Cardinals reach the World Series for the first time since 1987.

Down two runs early in Game 7, La Russa's charts apparently told him that Roger Clemens would not pitch out on the first pitch to Jeff Suppan, and the Cardinals pitcher squeezed home an important run.

In the eighth inning, La Russa trusted his gut and used Julian Tavarez against Carlos Beltran, who had homered off Tavarez to win Game 4 (before Tavarez took out his anger on a dugout telephone and broke fingers on his glove hand). La Russa could have gone with lefthander Ray King to turn Beltran around to his lesser-used right side, but La Russa won this gamble as Tavarez retired Beltran, Jeff Bagwell and Lance Berkman, another switch hitter.

The final regular-season game at old Busch Stadium draws a sign from Redbird fans John Olson and his son, Gabriel, of Coffeen, Ill.

OCT. 2 2005 GOODBYE TO BUSCH STADIUM

ONE OF MY FIRST MEMORIES OF BUSCH STADIUM was from about six blocks away. It was a Sunday evening on June 23, 1968, and I was to enlist in the Army the next day at the 12th and Spruce recruiting station.

As I left the barracks there to get a sandwich at a nearby White Castle, I could hear the noise from a crowd of 49,743 at Busch Stadium, which seemed to be having a lot of fun at a Sunday doubleheader (they had those then) between the Cardinals and the Atlanta Braves. Little did I know as I was about to sign my life away for three years that I would get to take part in that fun for more than 30 years myself as a sportswriter for the Post-Dispatch.

After the Army was only too happy to see me leave, I was hired by the Post-Dispatch in 1971 and a couple of years later, I got to cover my first game.

Not even knowing how to get into the clubhouse, I entered the park through the main entrance and hopped over the railing, hoping to interrogate a Montreal Expo or two as they engaged in batting practice.

I had heard of Boots Day before, inasmuch as he had played for the Cardinals. He was pleasant enough to talk to and not nearly as intimidating as the next Expo I encountered, all-business, all-the-time Gene Mauch, the Expos' manager, who had little time for my small talk.

From then on, the highlights — and lowlights — of covering ball at Busch were numerous.

There was laughter in seeing how the West Coast teams tried to deal with the heat of summertime as vapor trails rose from the artificial turf. With temperatures shooting to more than 140 degrees sometimes on the turf, you would see Padres or Giants or Dodgers players putting cabbage leaves in their hats. The Cardinals loved seeing the West Coast teams come to town in July, because it meant at least two victories in every three-game series.

There was sadness in seeing two funerals in a week's time at Busch in June 2002, when Hall of Fame broadcaster Jack Buck and ace pitcher

Fredbird plays chauffeur for former Cardinals shortstop Ozzie Smith during festivities at old Busch Stadium's regular-season swan song.

Darryl Kile died a few days apart.

There was disbelief in seeing Cardinals catcher Ted Simmons being ejected from a game just as he was about to step onto home plate after he had hit a game-tying homer off Chicago's Bruce Sutter in May 1978. It seems that Simmons had been disenchanted with a previous strike call by the home-plate umpire and let Paul Runge know about it on the way home.

There was head-scratching when Montreal coach Dave Bristol and Cardinals outfielder Reggie Smith got into a fight at the plate — while handing in the lineup cards — as the postscript to a disagreement the teams had the night before.

There were historic moments in abundance: A pair of 3000s — Bob Gibson's strikeout of Cesar Geronimo and Lou Brock's base hit off Dennis Lamp's leg. . . . A rare high fastball (82 miles an hour) by Cardinals reliever Sutter in the ninth inning of Game 7 of the 1982 World Series. The split-fingered specialist surprised Milwaukee batter Gorman Thomas and the Series was over. . . . Ozzie Smith's first lefthanded home run ever — a liner to right field in the ninth inning of Game 5 of the 1985 National League playoffs. Folks went crazy.

And there were oddities in abundance: Journeyman first baseman Mike Laga hitting a foul ball into a flower bed on Sept. 15, 1986. No big deal except that the flower bed was outside Busch Stadium and his foul ball was the only ball — fair or foul — to ever leave the stadium. . . . Montreal's David Palmer pitching a perfect game that wasn't. Palmer threw a five-inning perfect game, the second game of a doubleheader, which was called in the wee hours because of rain on April 21, 1984. It since has been stricken from the record books because it wasn't a nine-inning game. . . . Manager Tony La Russa valiantly trying to help the grounds crew control a wind-blown tarpaulin, only to lose his balance and fall to the ground during a storm delay in 2000. The tarp did not roll over him, as the automatic version did to the fastest

 Sisters Julie Scheaffer (left) of Oakville, Mo., and Lisa Deters of Lake of the Ozarks, Mo., are among those shedding tears over the stadium's demise.

▲ Albert Pujols' dramatic home run in Houston makes Game 6 possible, but the Astros stop him and the Cards to win the NLCS at Busch.

◄ The final regular-season game played at old Busch Stadium attracts fans in sundry kinds of garb.

Exuberant Houston pitchers Roger Clemens (left) and Roy Oswalt horse around after their team's pennant-winning victory in the final game at old Busch.

player alive, Vince Coleman, before Game Four of the 1985 National League Championship Series.

There was the "in-your-face" division title-clinching by the Cardinals against Montreal in 1987 as players from the hated New York Mets, the pursuers and the Cardinals' final regular-season opponents, watched from the press box. And there was the "in-your-face" scuffle between San

 Fans snap a flock of photos as the curtain comes down on the stadium.

▲ Not afraid to get down and dirty, fans scoop souvenir dirt from the first-base warning track.

Francisco and Cardinals players that wound up with managers Whitey Herzog and Roger Craig exchanging shoves.

There was Cardinals baserunner Ray Lankford knocking Philadelphia catcher Darren Daulton halfway into next week on a play at the plate that gave the Cardinals a ninth-inning victory in 1991. And Mark McGwire knocking a ball halfway to the Arch, a couple of hours after he had signed a long-term contract and then had broken down crying as he discussed his foundation to help victims of child abuse.

There was pure speed, as Brock stole a record 105th base in September 1974. And there was pure cunning, as backup catcher Glenn Brummer stole home in the 12th inning of a 1982 game to give the Cardinals a pennant-race victory over the Giants.

There were spectacular individual efforts with entire seasons on the line, like Jim Edmonds' diving catch to keep the Cardinals alive in Game 7 of the 2004 NLCS. Edmonds kept the Cardinals alive in that same NLCS

Stephanie Kluck of St. Charles, Mo., ventures into previously forbidden territory as she pays a visit to a men's restroom before leaving the stadium after the final game.

the night before, too, with a 12th-inning, game-winning homer off Houston's Dan Miceli.

And now, perhaps the best memory of all is yet to come. Oct. 26 and 27 are the scheduled dates for the fourth and fifth games of the World Series. If the Cardinals get that far, those will be the very last games at Busch. Many would think there probably would be no better way to send off this 39-year-old memory bank than to see the local nine taking a victory lap and the fans cavorting on a field that really won't have to be fixed up again.

Mark Mulder takes fellow pitcher Jason Marquis' truck for a spin in the outfield the day after the final game is played in the stadium.

COMMISH'S MOMENT

THE LAST REGULAR-SEASON GAME AT BUSCH STADIUM also marked the last pitch Al Reyes would throw for the Cardinals. The veteran reliever blew out his elbow cranking up a slider, and his loss was critical in the playoffs as the Cardinals lost the National League Championship Series to Houston.

My lasting memory of the day was the interaction the Cardinals' greats from different eras had with each other as they went to their various positions in a postgame ceremony. First base, for instance, was well occupied with Mark McGwire, Will Clark and Keith Hernandez.

The stadium's five remaining arches pose for a final photo before their demolition.

OCT. 27 2006 LA RUSSA AT THE PINNACLE

FOLKS AROUND HERE KNOW their Cardinals baseball managers by their first names. Red, Whitey, Joe, Tony. But that hasn't necessarily meant they all have been held in the same esteem.

Red Schoendienst, who grew up in Germantown, Ill., and has lived in the area his whole life, won one World Series (1967) as Cardinals manager and forever will be revered.

Dorrel Norman Elvert Herzog, who grew up in New Athens, Ill., and has lived in the area most of his life, won one World Series (1982) as Cardinals manager and forever will be revered.

Joe Torre, who grew up in New York and lives there today, has won four World Series, all with the Yankees. Part of the reason for his having no World Series wins here is that his best starting pitchers often were people such as Vicente Palacios and Donovan Osborne. Case closed. Torre is not quite as revered here as a manager, but his Most Valuable Player season of 1971, when he hit .363 with 137 runs batted in, will not be forgotten.

Then there is California resident Tony La Russa, who, completing his 11th season as Cardinals manager — the longest any Cardinals manager had gone without winning a World Series — finally has won one. That ties him with Schoendienst and Herzog on the Cardinals' hit parade and adds to the one he won in Oakland in 1989.

Surely, his reputation here this year has been enhanced by his ability to guide a talented yet flawed club through injury, illness and overzealous expectations. And then, when there were no delusions of a World Series title after the Cardinals backed into the National League Central Division title, La Russa and his team exceeded every expectation in what was a dream month of October.

With the Oakland championship in 1989 having occurred at a time

 Manager Tony La Russa has good reason to kick up his heels as he celebrates with general manager Walt Jocketty after the Cardinals win the World Series by beating Detroit in Game 5.

David Eckstein hits a broken-bat single to drive in a run in the second inning of Game 5.

Highly valued by La Russa for his defensive prowess, light-hitting catcher Yadier Molina turns into a tough out and helps the Cardinals win the World Series.

when the San Francisco Bay area still was recovering from a tragic earthquake, there was no champagne.

"Looming over it all is that people were killed and injured and there was loss of property," La Russa said. "It was a devastating hit to the Bay Area. We were careful not to celebrate. I've never been a part of a parade."

Now, after a five-game victory over the Detroit Tigers, there will be a parade — the first one here for baseball since Herzog's Cardinals beat Milwaukee in seven games in 1982 to win the Series.

And La Russa, ever mindful of Cardinals history, helped close it out with Hall of Famers Stan Musial (85 years old), Red Schoendienst (83), Bob Gibson (70) and Lou Brock (67) among those on hand.

Musial played on three World Series champions and was general manager of one (1967), Schoendienst played on two Cardinals World Series champions, coached for one and managed one. Brock and Gibson played on two World Series champions.

This is only one Cardinals' World Series title for La Russa, but the Hall of Famers applaud him as an equal.

Gibson, who enjoys verbal sparring with La Russa, said: "As far as I'm concerned, he's a damned good manager. At times, he can be very controlling as far as allowing guys to do what they know how to do.

"In some instances, I understood. In other instances, it was not so good.

But if it works, how are you going to say anything negative about it? If it doesn't work, there will be all kinds of things to say. That's human nature."

Gibson said he isn't sure how the average fan feels about La Russa, "but I don't think the average fan knows that much about it. That's why they call them fans. I think he's done a wonderful job with what he's had to work with. Period."

One longtime Cardinals front-office employee, who has seen 30 years' worth of managerial regimes here, said: "From what he's done, especially this year, Tony is now the standard. He's been in six postseasons here in seven years. Other managers should be compared to him, instead of comparing him to other managers.

"From four weeks ago, when we were about to go down in flames, to where we are now is almost incomprehensible."

Club president Mark Lamping, who was among those who flew to Scottsdale, Ariz., to hire La Russa after the 1995 season, said: "I love Whitey Herzog just like any Cardinal fan who went through 1982. Tonight Tony made his mark, but he made his mark a long time ago. It's a great day for him and his family."

Longtime Cardinals broadcaster and player Mike Shannon played for Schoendienst and followed Herzog and La Russa teams from the booth. He speaks highly of all three, but he is concerned that even with this world championship, "I don't think (La Russa) will be appreciated, to be quite honest."

Shannon said he thought that day might come, but after La Russa is gone.

"He falls into that category of greatness that won't be adorned until a time later on," Shannon said. "When people are in a position like that — presidents like (Harry) Truman, for instance — they're under such scrutiny that time is what proves their worth.

"I don't think you can put a finger on any one thing as to why it's that way with Tony. Maybe it's because of his so-called cerebral nature that he gets a lot more criticism than he should in this market."

Whatever the fans might feel, said Shannon, "I think the people who really understand the game know his worth, his greatness. And I think that's the supreme compliment. There's no doubt he's going into the Hall of Fame as a manager."

Shannon has been most impressed by La Russa's respect for his job with such a storied franchise.

"I think he holds managing the St. Louis Cardinals in reverence above everything else," Shannon said. "And there's no doubt in my mind he's wanted this world championship more than anything else he's wanted in his professional career."

 Adam Wainwright gets the game-ending strikeout and the Cardinals begin celebrating their World Series victory.

 Eckstein, the World Series MVP, is the life of the party at Busch.

 The Cardinals light up downtown on a chilly October night with a post-Series fireworks display.

With the franchise's 10th World Series title in hand, La Russa takes a moment to catch his breath before leaving his Busch Stadium office.

The focus is on the players, but loyal Cardinals fans like Diane Ceretto enjoy their own day in the sun at the victory parade.

No vantage point goes unused as the World Series parade makes its way through downtown St. Louis.

22ND JUDICIAL CIRCUIT
OF MISS

Chris Carpenter works the crowd as the Cardinals go on stage to be saluted as World Series champions.

A sea of red parts for the Cardinals as the parade ends and the party inside Busch begins.

Surrounded by thousands of fans dressed in Cardinal red, La Russa stands out by sporting a "Smooch Your Pooch!" T-shirt.

COMMISH'S MOMENT

THAT THE CARDINALS WON THE WORLD SERIES maybe shouldn't have been as great a national surprise as it appeared to be.

They wouldn't have made it to late October if they had to plow through the American League minefields, but they had to beat only one American League team, not several.

And that one team, the young Detroit Tigers, had been off for a week, hearing everyone tell them how good they were.

Once Anthony Reyes stifled the Tigers in Game One, the Series belonged to the Cardinals, the Tigers' almost comical defensive efforts notwithstanding.

TEMPY'S HIT RECORD

THE MOST NOTABLE OF MYRIAD GOINGS-ON in a twi-night double-header at Busch Stadium was that the Cardinals' Garry Templeton became the first player in recorded major-league history to achieve 100 hits from each side of the plate.

▲ Garry Templeton dashes into baseball's record book with a bunt single.

Templeton did it with a rare righthanded bunt single in the second game against the New York Mets. He was immediately whisked into a ceremony in which he was presented a plaque by the Cardinals and then whisked right out of the game after that.

It was back in early August when Templeton, studying a statistics sheet, noticed that he had 71 hits righthanded to go with 90 lefthanded. "I wonder if anybody ever has done it before," he mused. "I've got a chance."

As the season wound down to its final days, Templeton also batted righthanded against righthanders, going 6 for 15 (.400). Of his righthanded 100th, on a bunt against lefthander Pete Falcone, Templeton said "I'd been wanting to bunt all the time." But in the first game, he couldn't get it done against hard-throwing righthander Juan Berenguer "because he's so wild. I didn't know where the ball was going."

Once he achieved the 100-100 feat, Templeton said he didn't want to play in the season's final two games. "I'm not tired," he said, "but I've done all I can do."

EXTRA   OCT. 2, 1981

UNHAPPY ENDING

PITTSBURGH

IN MORE THAN A DOZEN YEARS OF CARDINALS BASEBALL, there has not been a more dramatic home run than the one Darrell Porter hit in the ninth inning of this game.

Only three nights earlier, fans at Busch Stadium celebrated the Cards taking over first place.

After George Hendrick had homered a few batters before to help the Cardinals climb back to a 7-6 deficit after they had trailed the Pittsburgh Pirates 7-2, Porter — on a 1-2 count with two outs — smashed a drive which just eased inside the right-field foul pole. Tie game, and although the first-place Montreal Expos had won their game, there still was hope among the second-place Cardinals.

"When Darrell hit the home run, it was the biggest lift we've had," said Tom Herr. "There was no way I thought we'd lose that game."

The Cardinals did lose 8-7. The victim was reliever Bruce Sutter, who allowed a walk to Omar Moreno to start the bottom of the ninth and then, after a sacrifice by Tim Foli and an intentional walk to Dave Parker, a ground-rule double to left-center by pinch-hitter Mike Easler.

Manager Whitey Herzog said he had made a quick exit from the dugout when the ball was hit. "I didn't even see it hit the ground," he said.

The loss put the Cardinals 1 1/2 games back of Montreal with just two games remaining in the second-half pennant race. While the defeat did not render the clubhouse into a tomb, it was suitably numbing.

Do you believe in miracles, Whitey? "No, not really," said Herzog. "Not too many of them."

EXTRA   **OCT. 15, 1982**

WONDROUS WILLIE

MILWAUKEE

THERE HAVE BEEN 79 WORLD SERIES involving some 400 games and almost 4,000 players. But Willie McGee, a Cardinals rookie with a penchant for excitement, daring and occasional anguish, had a game for the ages Friday night.

△ Lonnie Smith greets Willie McGee after the rookie's first World Series homer.

"I don't know if anybody ever played a World Series game better than he did," said manager Whitey Herzog after the Cardinals' 6-2 victory over the Milwaukee Brewers in the third game of the World Series.

McGee's first World Series hit was a three-run homer off former Cardinals pitcher Pete Vuckovich, breaking a scoreless tie in the fifth inning. His second hit was a solo home run, even farther to right field, in the seventh inning.

Meantime, he made an extraordinary leaping catch of Paul Molitor's drive to deep center in the first inning, and an almost incomprehensible home-run saving grab of Gorman Thomas' blast in the ninth.

McGee's leap on the second catch took his arm over the railing in front of the left-center field seats. The fence is 10 feet high.

"I'd like to know what Willie McGee's eating — Wheaties or what?" said Vuckovich.

McGee, searching for an explanation, said: "I don't believe I'm here. But, baseball is baseball. Anything can happen at any time."

EXTRA   OCT. 16, 1982

MILWAUKEE 'NIGHTMARE'

MILWAUKEE

PITCHER DAVE LAPOINT'S ERROR ON A ROUTINE PLAY opened the gates for the Milwaukee Brewers to score six unearned runs in the seventh inning — and a World Series the Cardinals should lead three games to one is tied, 2-2.

◀ The Brewers are feeling pretty good about themselves as they gain the upper hand in the 1982 World Series.

Milwaukee erased a 5-1 Cardinal lead to steal a 7-5 victory that reduced the Series to a best-of-three confrontation.

"We only needed one out," said Cardinals manager Whitey Herzog, "and seven straight hitters got on base."

The Cardinals blitzed the Brewers early with aggressive baserunning that included Willie McGee scoring from third and Ozzie Smith from second on the same sacrifice fly. Lefthanded rookie LaPoint was breezing toward Bruce Sutter time when Ben Oglivie hit a ball which took a high hop at first base. Keith Hernandez leaped to glove it and then tossed to LaPoint covering the bag. LaPoint dropped the ball and Oglivie was safe.

"I might have taken my eye off the ball to look at Oglivie," said LaPoint. "The ball hit me right here (he pointed to the palm of his glove)."

Herzog said, "LaPoint ran two steps for that ball. I don't know how he dropped it. It looked like an easy inning. It turned out to be a nightmare."

TERRIFIC TIMING

NEW YORK

THE NEW YORK METS HAVE BEEN CHASING the Cardinals for most of the summer, but when they finally arrived at the front door, Terry Pendleton and Tom Herr slammed it in their faces.

Terry Pendleton's clutch hitting helps the Cardinals survive a tough pennant race in 1987.

Held to one hit until two were out in the ninth inning and continuing their generally abysmal play, the Cardinals exploded for three runs, including a game-tying homer by Pendleton. Herr then snapped a nothing-for-21 slump with a go-ahead single in the 10th as the Cardinals beat the Mets 6-4.

Had the Cardinals lost, they would have risked forfeiting first place today in the National League Eastern Division, but now they are assured of leaving town still atop the division.

Trailing 4-1 with two out in the ninth, the Cardinals had a runner at second and still only one hit. "It didn't look very good," manager Whitey Herzog said.

But Willie McGee's single scored Ozzie Smith before Pendleton blasted his dramatic two-run homer over the center-field wall off Roger McDowell.

Pendleton said he never had tried for a home run this year until that at-bat. The first pitch was a foul strike. "The first sinker I pounded into the dirt," Pendleton said, "so I decided to move up (in the box) a little bit and see if I could catch one before it sank."

That six-inch moveup translated into 420 feet, and the Cardinals were back in a game they deserved to lose.

EXTRA   **OCT. 13, 1987**

KINGS OF THE HILL

JOHN TUDOR, TODD WORRELL AND KEN DAYLEY made the most of a threadbare Cardinals offense, and the Minnesota Twins still don't know whom they'll be playing in the World Series.

John Tudor returns a salute from the fans as he leaves a Game 6 thriller against the Giants.

A misplay by San Francisco right fielder Candy Maldonado led to a second-inning run, and the three Cardinals pitchers clung to that lead like their last $5 bill as the Cardinals evened the National League Championship Series at three games apiece with a 1-0 victory.

Tudor held the Giants to six hits for 7 ⅓ innings before yielding to Worrell, who got three outs. Then, Cardinals manager Whitey Herzog got to pull his pet pitcher-to-right-field trick in the ninth when left-handed-hitting Harry Spilman was announced as a pinch-hitter. Herzog brought in lefthander Dayley and moved Worrell to right field, and Dayley got the final two outs.

A sellout crowd of 55,331 became a mite overzealous in its treatment of Giants left fielder Jeffrey Leonard, the people's choice at Busch Stadium.

Leonard was serenaded with chants of "Jeff-REY. Jeff-REY." But Leonard also had to dodge cowbells, empty cups, full cups and coins. Left-field umpire Eric Gregg said, "I got 75 cents in change."

San Francisco manager Roger Craig said the situation was such that he was ready to take his team off the field. Home-plate umpire Bob Engel said he had told the Giants "that if Jeffrey felt threatened, he could come in and I'd take the team off the field."

EXTRA   **MAY 16, 1998**

LEAVING HIS MARK

JUST WHEN YOU'RE ALMOST SURE YOU'VE SEEN all Mark McGwire has to offer, the Cardinals' first baseman amazes even more.

Four days after launching the longest measured home run in Busch Stadium history, 527 feet, McGwire hit a ball off Florida's Livan Hernandez an estimated 545 feet. It banged off the Post-Dispatch sign in deepest center field, well above the green hitting backdrop and dangerously close to people in party rooms who never thought they would have to scramble to safety.

McGwire, who has hit three 500-foot-plus homers here and had a 538-foot drive off Randy Johnson in Seattle last year, said this home run was "the best ball I've ever hit. I don't think I could hit a better one."

Mark McGwire connects for the longest measured homer in Busch Stadium history: 545 feet.

Cardinals third baseman John Mabry suggested that if the sign hadn't stopped the ball in its tracks, "it would have hit the roof at Pop's (a nightclub across the Mississippi River in Sauget). Or Johnny's Famous Chili in Soulard."

Florida coach Rich Donnelly, who is expected to throw batting practice to McGwire during the home-run contest at the All-Star Game, called this effort "stupid."

"I saw people in the upper deck ducking," Donnelly said. "You'd think a guy who has hit his longest home run would pull it. But this was to straightaway center. If he ever pulls one — and this is completely absurd — he may hit one out of the park."

EXTRA **JUNE 25, 1999**

NO WAY, JOSE

THE CHANCE THAT JOSE JIMENEZ would win this matchup — he had one victory in his last 11 starts — was remote, let alone the absurd possibility he would throw a no-hitter.

Upon returning to Busch Stadium, Jose Jimenez is honored for the no-hitter he pitched in Arizona.

But with the help of two dazzling plays by Cardinals right fielder Eric Davis, one of them in the ninth inning, Jimenez not only outdueled Arizona ace Randy Johnson but tossed the first no-hitter in the major leagues by a rookie since 1991 when he silenced the Diamondbacks 1-0.

"Unbelievable. I can't explain it," a euphoric Jimenez said. "I just want to fly right now."

Jimenez was handled masterfully by Alberto Castillo, even though he often found himself being yelled at by his catcher. "He'd say, 'Come on.' I'd say, 'You come on. I'm ready,'" said Jimenez.

Asked how he could have improved so much from recent starts, Jimenez said, "I was working on my mechanics. I think I'm back."

Later, Jimenez will shoot higher. "My goal is to be a superstar," he said.

EXTRA   **SEPT. 2, 2001**

NO-HIT SURPRISE

SAN DIEGO

THOSE WHO WITNESSED THE BUD SMITH-BOBBY JONES pitching matchup last week in St. Louis, a fiasco won by Smith's Cardinals 16-14,

▲ Reporters pounce on rookie Bud Smith as he leaves the field after pitching a no-hitter.

would have been caught completely off-guard this time.

While San Diego's Jones was a little better, lefthanded rookie Smith was unfathomable. After giving up 14 earned runs in his previous 14 innings, Smith gave up nothing — runs or hits — as he no-hit the Padres 4-0.

Pitching coach Dave Duncan said that, as Smith's pitch count had reached 70 through five innings, he thought there was no way the lefthander could go nine. "I was almost rooting for him to give up a hit so we could get him out of there," Duncan said.

Smith admitted he was pitching on fumes at the end. "You're starting to get a little fatigued in the sixth, seventh, eighth and you're saying, 'I need to get my adrenaline back.' "

But all night, until Tony Gwynn came to bat amid a standing ovation in the eighth, Smith was so focused that he said, "I couldn't hear anybody in the stands."

EXTRA   **OCT. 14, 2001**

BATTING FOR McGWIRE

PHOENIX

MARK McGWIRE, A SAD STORY FOR MOST OF THE SEASON, wound up the National League playoffs no better than his .187 average during the regular season.

Mark McGwire sits alone in the Cardinals dugout after being replaced in his final game.

Still beset by his ailing right knee, McGwire struck out three times in three at-bats against Arizona righthander Curt Schilling. Manager Tony La Russa then pinch-hit for McGwire in the ninth inning of a tie game, asking rookie Kerry Robinson to sacrifice. La Russa was almost in anguish at having to pinch-hit for McGwire, who has 583 home runs in his career.

"One of my lowest moments as a manager was pinch-hitting for Mark," La Russa said. "But you've got to try to win the game."

Recently, McGwire had said his mind was "fried," and he again talked about re-evaluating his future in the offseason. Could this have been his last game?

"There's a chance," he said. "Like I said, I'm going to sit back and think about things. Your body can only go far. I'll probably let you guys know through fax or e-mail."

PHOTOGRAPHY CREDITS

Post-Dispatch photographers
Gary Bohn: 84, 87
David Carson: 4
Robert Cohen: 172, 176
Wayne Crosslin: 109, 149
Andy Cutraro: 74, 76, 159
Noah Devereaux: 204
Scott Dine: 21
Karen Elshout: 146, 210
J.B. Forbes: 12, 17, 22, 25, 26. 30, 33, 50, 56, 58, 59, 60, 62, 67, 72, 81, 92, 94, 170, 171, 188, 189, 192, 203, 215, 218
Robert C. Holt III: 105
Robert LaRouche: 68, 102
Chris Lee: 7, 9, 152, 154, 157, 158, 162, 163, 164, 166, 177, 179, 180, 181, 193, 196, 200, 206, 211, 221, 223
Huy Richard Mach: 186, 190, 191, 209
Kevin Manning: 64, 130, 144
Odell Mitchell, Jr.: 91, 96, 134, 147, 150, 220
Jerry Naunheim, Jr.: 112, 142
Wes Paz: 98, 100, 106, 108, 110
Jane Rudolph: 128
Laurie Skrivan: 136, 139, 174, 194, 198, 202, 208, 212
Gabriel Tait: 182, 184, 185
Dilip Vishwanat: 132
Larry Williams: 34

Post-Dispatch files: 15, 55

Other photographers
Associated Press: 18, 38, 46, 78, 88, 116, 120, 124, 214, 216, 217, 219
Bettman/Corbis: 52
Charles Bennett, Associated Press: 160
Lenny Ignelzi, Associated Press: 222
St. Louis Cardinals: 37
Scott Rovak, St. Louis Cardinals: 169
Kansas City Star: 70
United Press International: 42

Back cover photo by **Chris Lee**